Becky's Bloomers

a garden year in the Northland

Rebecca Livermore

Loonfeather Press
Bemidji, Minnesota

Cover by Mary Lou Marchand
Photos by Brian Livermore
First Printing, 2005
Printed in Canada by Hignell Book Printing
ISBN 0-926147-19-6

This publication is printed on 100% recycled paper.

Loonfeather Press is a not for profit small press organized under section
501 (c) (3) of the United States Internal Revenue Code

Loonfeather Press
P.O. Box 1212
Bemidji, MN 55619
USA

Dedication

This book is dedicated with love and thanks to my mom, Clara Vesledahl Martin, and to the memory of my dad, Harold Martin, who were farmers on the edge of the Red River Valley, and who passed on to me their love for the land and what it grows.

This book is also for my husband Brian, who has always supported me with love, enthusiasm, and humor.

ACKNOWLEDGMENTS

Life happens. Sometimes we have direct input, and other times it seems that we don't. Becoming a gardening "advisor," writing newspaper columns and ultimately authoring a book were not part of my life's plans way back when. I completed college with the intent of making a career of teaching high school students. But when we decided to live in Canada and from there, Michigan and Iowa, where my teaching license didn't apply, my life took a turn and my days in front of the classroom were ended.

When we returned to Minnesota in the mid-80s, the Master Gardener program with the University of Minnesota Extension was in full swing. I took the training in Beltrami County and fulfilled volunteer hours, in part, by writing for a local daily newspaper. It was a year later that a publisher of a free weekly community newspaper contacted me and asked me to write a folksy garden column full of anecdotes and advice. His name is George Williams, and he and his wife, Linda, started me out on what was to be 13 years of writing and meeting gardeners from all across the area. At my husband's suggestion, we called the column Becky's Bloomers, and if I had a quarter for every time someone asked me how my bloomers were, I'd be rich! Without the Williams' confidence in me, and their encouragement every writing season as they told of readers asking for my column, this book would never have been written. My thanks to them both for sticking by me those 13 years and giving me an opportunity of a lifetime. Mary Lou Marchand with the Loonfeather Board has been my faithful advisor and friend these past months, and her assistance in getting me to the point of publication has been invaluable. I had no idea of the book publishing process other than the writing itself, and she led me gently along the way.

Another person I wish to thank is an old gardening friend Darryl Lauderbaugh, who, with his wife of many years, has the most beautiful garden on Roosevelt Road. Every time I would see them in the grocery store or garden center, he would ask how my book was coming and when it would be out for them to buy. He was a greater inspiration than he'll ever know, and much like my conscience, Darryl let me know in his friendly way that I had to get busy and put this book together. Thank you, Darryl, for prodding me along and reminding me that time waits for no one!

Finally, I have my husband Brian to thank not only for his wizardly computer expertise and photography skills, but also for his creative insight and advice which he gave without hesitation. If I had his imagination and fearless technological talent, I'd be dangerous. I'll long remember the windy summer afternoon out west in farming country where he perched on a ladder among the sunflowers with his camera clicking away. The result is on the back cover of this book where I'm actually waving at a farmer I know driving past in his combine. It was a great day together, and I'm looking ahead to years more of them.

AUTHOR'S NOTES

I am a farm girl at heart. Never mind the fact that we lived the first fifteen years of our married life in big cities. In my hopes and dreams, we would always end up living in rural America, ideally someplace in the friendly Midwest. And here we are thirty years later, in a log house nestled among the woods on the banks of the Mississippi in northern Minnesota. It's a dream come true, for the most part. At times I feel a bit claustrophobic, encircled by these mature aspen, birch and pine. The only cure is an afternoon's drive toward the west and familiar open country where I can see the horizons, both east and west, at the same time. I open the car window all the way down, prop my elbow on the ledge, and breathe in the fresh air from the wide open spaces. Brought up on the edge of the prairie, we were able to see at least a mile in every direction, farther if we climbed up the windmill ladder which, of course, was off-limits to us kids. Those were glory days on the small farm in the mid-50s. All farms were small back then, and every farmer grew what it took to live, including grain to sell and alfalfa to feed the numerous animals.

Seasons and their changes were evident on the farm. Routine dictated how we adapted to each change, whether it was in chores to be done, crops to be put in or plowed under, gardens to turn over, or clothes to be readied for school. Gardening was a distant concern for me. In fact, it was practically non-existent. Mom always had a huge garden which kept us busy weeding, picking and canning, but it was on the bottom of my list of favorite things to do. There's no doubt that, even though I disliked it at the time, this was the beginning of my need to plant things and watch them grow. Many years passed quickly by, and it wasn't until I was married that the yearning to return to my farming roots and the interest in gardening once again took hold.

As I add years to my life, it becomes more clear to me that, as with gardens, our lives mature through each season. We begin life with vigor, energy, curiosity and optimism, exactly the way I look forward to every gardening experience in the spring. By the time fall rolls around, I'm more content to savor the accomplishments and look ahead to the quiet time of winter. This coincides with my attitudes now that I'm well into mid-life and contemplating the more golden years of adulthood. There are still bridges to cross, adventures to seek, and accomplishments to number, but they become less demanding and more gentle in nature. My intent in writing this short book is not only to give suggestions that may help your gardening experiences, but also to reflect on my life, and perhaps yours, as a journey through the seasons, with each season unique and wonderful in its own right. I hope you find value in both.

CONTENTS

Spring ❧

Spring ❧

Spring is slow in coming to the Northland. Or so it seems. Maybe it's like Christmas is for children. The anticipation and eagerness make the time crawl by until finally spring arrives. I could usually smell spring's arrival on the farm, well ahead of the actual weather change. The wind carrying the stink of rotting manure from behind the barn was a sure indication that the thaw was here and winter was about over. Sounds were different, too. Birds were louder and more numerous; in the pasture milk cows kicked up their heels and bawled with pleasure as they celebrated their release from the small barn. All creatures announced their survival from the long, cold winter. We kids donned boots and tramped through mud puddles and climbed into the haymow to check on the newly born kittens. All around us life took on a new attitude.

And so it continues in my gardening life today, many years later. Spring is the time for new beginnings, making changes that we deem important. Gardening gives us the chance to put these yearnings and plans to work. Our fingers almost seem to itch with the desire to dig in the dirt, to feel the texture of the earth that supports plant life and emits the damp, cool smell so full of promise. The process of sowing seeds, watching them sprout and grow into productive plants remains a miraculous phenomenon to me, one I anticipate eagerly each spring.

This annual rite is one way I keep in touch with Nature, synonymous with Creator in my book. I remember seeing a sign in a friend's garden that reads "I'm always nearer to God when I'm in my garden," or something on that order. The need to nurture is a strong pull that yanks us out of our easy chairs and into the outdoors at any hour of the day or night, come rain or come shine. What will thrive in our gardens this year? Which seeds germinated in five days and which ones didn't come up at all? Should I expand my flower garden and give up on summer squash that took up too much room last year? Is there anything the deer won't eat? All of these decisions and experiments await my call. I wouldn't give up this time of year for anything! If only it would linger awhile longer. . .

SUGAR TIME AND OTHER RITES OF SPRING

The sap's running, and that's not a political statement! I'm talking about maple sap and the popular North Country process called "sugaring off."

In areas where soil is heavier and maple trees abound, many locals have been grabbing their pails and bringing in sap to boil down into delicious maple syrup. Cool nights followed by warm days bring on the flow of sap. The first sap of the season that starts to run after nights have been the coldest is usually thought to be the best sap. Last week we were on the receiving end of a fresh jar of syrup from a patient friend of my husband. Was it good on top of a batch of home made waffles! But I'd much rather eat it and cook with it than go to all the work of making the syrup.

For instance, did you know that it takes 35 to 40 gallons of sap to make just one gallon of syrup? That's a lot of bucket hauling! The boil-down process is time consuming and tedious. Most sugarers have an outdoor sugar shack where they can build a big wood fire and boil away until the watery sap turns into golden-hued syrup. It's not a good idea to boil sap down in your house since it takes forever and puts out so much steam.

For those of us who end up buying our maple syrup from grocery shelves, we will find it labeled one of four categories. US Grade A Light Amber is the most delicate syrup. It is THE fancy syrup to use over ice cream, cake, French toast and waffles. Of course it's the most expensive, but when taste really counts, reach for this syrup because it's the best! US Grade A Medium Amber has a richer, darker color and more distinct maple flavor. It's considered an all-purpose syrup for cooking, marinades and glazes. US Grade A Dark Amber has a deep, rich color and caramel/woodsmoke flavor. A small quantity will add a distinct maple flavor, a little dash'll do ya! US Grade B, almost never seen on our local shelves, is used exclusively for baking.

If we store maple syrup in the refrigerator or a cool, dark place, it will keep for a long time, unless your family is as crazy about it as we are! It doesn't collect any dust or mold in our house!

If you need to prune back any oaks in your yard and just haven't had time to get at it yet, wait until after mid-July to prevent the spread of oak wilt by the oak bark beetle. Oak wilt isn't a big problem for us yet, so let's keep it that way. If oaks are accidentally damaged this time of year and must be trimmed, use a tree wound dressing right away.

Test old seeds you saved from last year before planting them in your garden. Put 10 seeds in a thick layer of damp paper towels. Roll up the towels, place them in a plastic bag and set the bag in a warm place (on top of the refrigerator is a good spot). Wait a few days and check the seeds. The number of seeds that sprout will tell you if it's worth your time to plant them this spring. Sometimes it's a good idea to plant old seeds generously. Don't skimp! If they all germinate, then we'll just have to do some thinning. I have half a package of bean seeds left over from two years ago so now's a good time to see if they'll sprout.

Speaking of beans, have you ever heard of an inoculant for legumes such as peas and beans? It is a dry, peat-based culture of beneficial bacteria for treating seeds of these legumes before planting time. It encourages the formation of high nitrogen nodules on plant roots for bigger plants and higher yields. It looks like dirt and is easy to use. Soak your seeds overnight. Drain off the moisture the next day and sprinkle some inoculant over the seeds. Roll the seeds around to make sure they're covered well. Then just plant as usual. Inoculant is good for only one year, so don't plan to use any you may have left over from last year. Always buy a fresh supply. It's on sale at all nurseries and garden centers this time of year.

Be really careful when you clean out your perennial gardens. It's so easy to damage some of the slow-starting, tender plants when we start digging around in the dirt in early spring. A tender touch is always the best.

I've got a use for all the dog hair floating around our floors this spring. I'll sweep it up and put it around some early perennials to see if it helps keep rabbits and squirrels away. Critter control is always a concern for us gardeners and if there's a benefit to this spring molting of our dogs, so much the better! To tell you the truth, I haven't seen many rabbits hopping around yet. Maybe the winter was too cruel with too many hungry foxes.

Keep this in mind when buying perennials for your flower gardens. Most have a blooming time of just 2 to 4 weeks. Then the curtain falls! But remember that the foliage of a plant can be as important to an attractive garden as the blooms. Look for perennials that have color and texture in their leaves. Some of my favorites are mounds of coral bells, peonies, bleeding hearts (they tend to yellow later on in summer), hosta and hardy geraniums (not to be confused with annual greenhouse geraniums). Russian sage (Perovskia) is also stunning, but it's tall so put it to the back of your perennial gardens.

COMPOST MAKES GARDENERS' GOLD

Now is the perfect time to start a compost pile. We have to clean up our messy yards this time of year anyway, so instead of jamming the leaves and small twigs into plastic bags, put them in a heap and do our landfills a favor. RECYCLE is the "catchword" these days. We gardeners can recycle organic waste materials into garden treasure easily. If we read too much about composting though, it will boggle our minds. All the fancy phrases can make a simple procedure seem confusing and overwhelming.

Compost is basically decomposed plant material. Anything that isn't plant material shouldn't be included in our compost heaps. What can we include? Just about anything from our kitchens EXCEPT grease, dairy products, meat scraps, newspapers, left-over tuna noodle casserole or dried out chocolate chip cookies (this never happens at our house!). In short, we can include all fruit and vegetable wastes. I keep an empty half-gallon milk carton under the sink and put in all coffee grounds, carrot and potato peels, orange and grapefruit skins, egg shells, cabbage cores, etc. I'm absolutely amazed at how quickly I fill this container! Then I take it to my compost pile, dump it on, mix it into the top layer so it's covered, sprinkle on some dirt and come back to the kitchen for another cup of coffee.

Where should you put your compost pile? Out of sight is probably a good answer! Mine is within 15 feet of my garden for a reason. When it's decomposed, it will not be such a chore to carry it to the garden where it will be used. Some gardeners compost right inside their garden plots for this same reason. Folks who have more limited space may need to start their heap hidden behind the garage, or along the back fence. Compost heaps can sometimes be an unsightly mess so keep your neighbor in mind and plan accordingly. I was surprised to find that my compost pile didn't generate an offensive odor. Of course, I didn't get too close to those rotting tomatoes from last fall! My heap did house a family of field mice last season, but they didn't eat much, and other than give me a scare now and then, I didn't mind their company. Most animals like stray dogs and weasels aren't attracted to a pile of vegetables. They're after meat scraps!

You will want to keep your compost heap contained in some way, especially if you're short of space. You can get some complex plans that would keep a building contractor happy for a few days, or you can do it the easy way by using materials you have on hand. One simple container is made with sturdy wire mesh that's 4 feet high and about 10 feet long. Form a cylinder by bringing the ends together and fastening them with wire. You can use left-over concrete blocks (with holes open) to form a 4-foot high 3-sided structure. Old hay bales make a good container. Although they take up more space, the added plus of using them is that eventually you can add them to your compost heap as well. If you use a large garbage can or drum, you'll need to puncture holes in the sides and bottom for drainage and air circulation. Whatever you decide to use, keep in mind that air needs to get at that compost so it will decay well.

So now you're ready with your heap of raked leaves, your bucket of coffee grounds and egg shells, and your mesh container. What next? Start layering. Begin with a forkful of leaves; pour on a layer of your kitchen waste; sprinkle on some all-purpose garden fertilizer which will speed up the decomposing process; top this with some soil from your garden. Keep layering until your pile is about 3 to 4 feet high. Wet it all down with your garden hose until it's moist but not slushy. That's all there's to it! In roughly 3 to 4 months, this mixture will break down and become dark and crumbly.

Be patient! However, you can hurry up the process by doing these things. Increase the amount of air in the pile by turning it about twice a month. Poke holes in it with a large pipe. Keep your pile at least 3 feet high and 3 feet wide. This is the minimum amount of decaying materials that will maintain an inside temperature high enough to kill off disease-causing organisms. The smaller the pieces of matter added to the pile, the faster it will decompose. This means you'll want to cut up that grapefruit before adding it to the pile. Mulched leaves also decay faster than those left whole. Once your heap is starting to decay, it's best not to add any fresh organic matter or it will slow down the process. If you have space, keep two compost piles, one of materials already decomposing, one for fresher materials. If you have some lime on your garden shelves, dust a bit of it on the layer of leaves and vegetable scraps. In addition to speeding up the decomposition, it also helps neutralize high acid build-up. Spring and summer rains may be enough to keep your heap moist. If it's a dry season, you'll need to add water every few days.

There are some items that should not be put in a compost pile. These include pet feces and leaves or fruit from diseased plants, as they may contain harmful bacteria that won't be killed off in the composting process. Also keep dairy products and any meat or bones out of the compost pile as they will attract carnivorous animals and raccoons and skunks—critters that don't make good neighbors!

TOOL TIME

"Use the right tool for the job," my husband chides me as I pry off a jar lid with an old kitchen knife. He's right, of course! The same holds true for garden tools. Some are positively essential to good gardening. Others are useful but not so important. One thing I have discovered through experience: cheap tools fall apart! Now I always look for well-made tools which usually means I have to open my wallet widely!

Four years ago I made one of the best garden tool investments of my life. After relying year after year on my neighbor's good will, I bit the bullet and bought my own garden tiller. It's not a big, fancy macho machine, but a small 20-pound gas-powered tiller that I can carry on one arm— and I love it!

I have a confession to make. Before this dandy machine arrived through the mail, I'd never used one of these small tillers. This isn't normally the way I buy things. Usually I check with *Consumers' Report*, then gather information and opinions from wise and experienced friends, then study all available facts, and only THEN do I reach the inevitable conclusion to buy the blamed thing. This time I was lured by the convincing ads that said, "Money back if not fully satisfied!" And I have had no regrets.

While I had no previous experience with one of these mini-tillers, I've had plenty with the bigger jumping bronco machines and have not been overly impressed. These machines shake a body's brains out of place! I've often thought it must be easier to train a pair of mules. My neighbor's rear-tine tiller that he pulls behind his garden tractor is top-notch. In no time flat he has several neighbors' gardens loose, fluffy and weed-free. This tiller is worth a small fortune, and many of us gardeners hesitate to make such a major investment. Hence I took the cheaper route by purchasing a tiller that cost a lot less, and more importantly, one that I can easily start and handle.

Believe it or not, this 20-pound tiller has a lot of power. The notion that, in order to work, a tiller needs weight and lots of engine muscle is just baloney. This small tiller with its stinky 2-cycle engine churns like crazy and digs as deeply as its more expensive relatives. And since it's so lightweight and easy to handle, it's perfect for those smaller jobs including raised beds. It starts like a snap, takes up little storage space and needs only a bit of routine maintenance. The interesting thing about these small tillers is that they work best if guided backwards, much like a vacuum cleaner. This isn't as awkward or stupid as it sounds. It's easy to see where you've been and once the soil is churned up; the gardener isn't tramping it down right away.

Good hand tools are just as necessary for us gardeners. One of the most useful to me is a short-handled cultivator that looks like a 3-pronged claw. With one of these in my hand, I'm a dangerous foe to any weeds daring to poke above ground. Of course I have to be on my knees, close to the plants and soil to use it, but my knees are stronger than my back so I don't mind the effort. I'm in the market this season for a new long-handled cultivator. Ever since our move last summer, I can't find my old one. Either it's propped up in a dark corner of the garage or it was sold at my rummage sale! If so, I hope I got lots of money for it! But it's no great loss. It was a cheap tool in the first place and needed to be replaced. Lesson #1: In most things we get what we pay for. This is certainly true with most garden tools.

Old-time gardeners wouldn't be caught dead without a hoe. It's a dependable basic tool, depending on who's on the other end of the handle, with a sharp edge that's deadly on weeds. It also makes furrows for planting and is good for hilling dirt around plants. Hoes come in various shapes geared for different jobs. Another sharp-edged tool that I really like has a short handle and is used to slice weeds off at the soil surface. I'm not sure of its name, but the blade is about 4 inches across and it's perfect for getting rid of small weeds that haven't sprawled all over.

Of course any gardener worth her/his salt has a trusty spade for cutting and moving soil from one place to another. And most of us wouldn't part with our gardening forks that we depend on for lifting clumps of dirt, overgrown perennials and hills of potatoes. But have you ever used a broadfork? This tool is used for lifting and turning soil that was prepared last season and is now compacted by the weather and numerous critter feet. It is easier and better to use for this purpose than a common garden fork due to its large size.

A broadfork, also called a U-Bar, has two long handles and 5 or 6 tines attached to a horizontal crossbar. The tines are anywhere from 10 to 18 inches long. To use this fork, we hold it upright, step up and onto the crossbar so the tines are pushed down into the ground. A pair of sturdy work boots is not an option but a requirement for this task! We then step off the crossbar and pull the handles toward us until the tines lift out of the soil. Working backwards at 6 inch intervals, this tool will loosen and aerate soils without the need for tilling or spading.

Having a good resting and hanging place for tools is almost as important as having the tools themselves. A garage or shed wall with hooks for hanging rakes, hoes, spades and forks will keep them in one place so we don't have to search all over when we need to use one. They'll also stay in better condition when not left outdoors in the rain, and bare feet will be safe from ambush by a sharp fork in the grass. Keep tools in good shape by cleaning them occasionally, and sand and paint worn wooden handles to avoid splinters in unprotected hands.

RHUBARB RULES

What vegetable grows on long, reddish-green stalks, is first up in the spring, and makes my husband's favorite pie? You guessed it—rhubarb. This native of Asia which was used there primarily for medicinal purposes was brought to our country in the late 1700s. Some of you probably wish it had stayed there! There's no middle ground when it comes to rhubarb. Either you love it or you can't stand the stuff! Regardless of how you feel about it, rhubarb flourishes in our part of the country where we have cool, often moist summers and winters cold enough to freeze out most other perennials. A friend of my mother's tells about the spring she packed two bags to take on a trip to Arizona: one bag held her clothing and personal things; the other was packed full of rhubarb! She had never before received such a hearty welcome from her northern-born relatives who were starved for the taste of fresh rhubarb. So you see, the Southwest may have lemons, strawberries and prickly pear cactus, but we are blessed with rhubarb!

From a cook's point of view, nothing could be easier to add to desserts, jams, sauces and relishes than rhubarb. There's no peeling, no seeds to take out, no bugs to wash off (rhubarb is amazingly pest and disease free). Rhubarb is a good source of vitamin A and contains some vitamin C and potassium. It's also low in calories. But by the time we add enough sugar to make it palatable, all of that advantage is gone with the wind! Eating raw rhubarb was a treat for my sister and me when we lived on the farm. Off to the garden we'd rush, cupped hands filled with sugar, and there we'd yank out a tart, red stem that made us pucker in spite of the sugary dip. It's that tartness that makes rhubarb so special. If a bite of pie doesn't make my husband hurt a little behind the ears (he says it's the parotid gland that does this), then it's too sweet!

Rhubarb is at its best this time of year. Mounds of it line neighbors' boundaries and gardens, enough to share with friends and neighbors and then some. It grows well in any well-drained fertile soil. The sandy loam commonly found in our area produces good rhubarb if we add compost, aged manure and fertilizers each year. As with most garden plants, rhubarb needs full sun and a constant water supply. A drought might be to blame for the hollow stems some gardeners find. Wait until the third year before you pick newly-planted rhubarb. By that time it has matured and become strong enough so that you can continue to harvest from the plant until the first part of July. After July when the hot, dry weather descends, the stalks lose flavor and become tough. The stem does not become poisonous. It just isn't as tasty.

The best way to pick rhubarb is by pulling it out. Don't cut it off. Grasp the stalk near the base and pull upward and to the side. Then cut or break off the leaf. These enormous leaves contain oxalic acid which is poisonous so don't plan to use them for anything other than your compost pile. Try not to pull more than a third of the stalks from a plant at any given time. If you pull too many, the crown may lack strength to keep producing well. Remove the flower stalks as soon as they appear. Otherwise the plant will send all of its food into the flower and forget about making new leafstalks.

The best time to plant root divisions and crowns of rhubarb is in the early spring before the leaves have shot up. As rhubarb becomes older, the stalks will become noticeably smaller each year. This usually means that it's time to divide the plant and start it again in a new, well-prepared spot. Often if we're in the right place at the right time, a neighbor who is dividing older plants will share a division with us. Remember this next winter and make plans to visit that neighbor in the spring.

If you're too busy to use your rhubarb after you've picked it, don't panic. Rhubarb stores well, unwashed and in a plastic bag, in the refrigerator for at least a week. It's a breeze to freeze rhubarb. Just wash the stalks, cut them into 1/2 to 1 inch pieces, and put them in containers or plastic bags. You can save the sugar for cooking time as rhubarb freezes well without it.

To keep my four hills of rhubarb healthy, I cover them with manure each fall before the snow flies. Since I don't have a cow, I purchase manure in 40-pound bags. Two bags will easily cover these four mounds and not only provide nutrients but protect the crowns from the winter chill.

PASS THE PEAS PLEASE

My Dad was a typical, no-nonsense dairy and grain farmer who wouldn't let a vegetable touch his plate unless it was peas, carrots or beans. For variety sometimes he'd like peas, beans or carrots. I didn't know what broccoli or cauliflower looked like until I went away to college. President Bush would have loved supper at our house! Needless to say, my sister and I spent what seemed like a zillion hours each summer picking and podding peas from my mother's huge garden. This was no job for a glamour-seeking teenager! I quickly learned to hate peas. In fact, podding peas ranked right up there with washing hens' eggs as the chore I hated the most. Fortunately, since those adolescent days I've had a complete turnabout. I can't imagine a vegetable garden without peas.

It's much easier and more fun to grow peas these days because they don't all have to be podded. I think the best-tasting ones available to us gardeners today are the newer snap peas. They are delicious when picked at almost any stage. Early on while the peas are just teeny bumps in the pods, they are tasty stir-fried, dipped, or added to casseroles and salads. As they mature, the entire pods can be snapped into bite-sized pieces, cooked and eaten, pods and all.

Every book on gardening that I've ever seen says to plant peas as soon as the ground can be worked in the spring. I often wonder what this means up here in the frigid North. No seed is going to sprout if the soil is less than 50 degrees. Even if we want to beat the heat and get those cool loving plants harvested before July, the seeds will just sit and rot in the ground if it's too cold. The only sure way to judge soil temperature is with a thermometer. Most of us just dig into our soil and guess. I've been using this tried and untrue method, often without success, so a soil thermometer is on my shopping list these days.

Peas produce the best in full sun. They like fertile, loamy and well-drained soil. The loamy sand in my garden is okay as long as I add organic matter each year. Don't over-fertilize peas. Too much nitrogen fertilizer will only make plants with lots of foliage and few peas. It's a good idea to dust your pea seeds with innoculant before planting. This legume innoculant, which looks like powdery dirt, adds nitrogen-fixing bacteria to the seeds, which helps increase the yield and quality of the plants. Our local garden centers carry it. Some gardeners soak their pea seeds overnight before planting so they will germinate faster. Others say this only makes the seeds rot more quickly in the ground. It probably depends on the particular pea cultivar, the condition of the soil, and our ever unpredictable weather. Since moist seeds collect more innoculant than dry seeds, I soak my peas for a half-hour, drain them, and then shake them around in the innoculant. Then I'm ready to plant.

I always keep extra seeds on hand to fill in where seeds haven't sprouted. This year I'm trying something different with my pea crop. Instead of planting them in double rows, I'm going to scatter seeds in a 5-foot square. Then I'll cover them with 2 inches of soil (one inch is enough in heavier soils) and hope for the best. If all goes as planned, the peas will support themselves. This will work only with the shorter peas. Those that vine 3-6 feet will need vertical support of some kind. If you have time, put up your pea supports before you plant. You'll find that it's much easier and less damaging to your plants than trying to position the supports after the peas are up and vining. The English have a great idea. Instead of using purchased supports that not only cost money but often stand out like a sore thumb, they use small leafless branches/twigs from nearby trees. These supports are quickly covered by growing peas and don't look out of place in a garden. Mulch peas and other cool weather plants with grass clippings, straw or wood shavings. Mulch will keep the roots cool and also prevent moisture from evaporating quickly. This means we'll have to water less often when the hot days of July arrive.

Rabbits love peas! I plan to beat them to the crop by using 2-foot chicken wire. It's easy to install. All we do is unwind enough to enclose bunny's favorite delectables—peas, broccoli and beans. A short pole placed every 4 feet is usually enough to keep the chicken wire upright. Hopefully this will keep me from uttering nasty words about rabbits this spring.

For the best taste around, plan to eat peas as soon as you've picked them from your garden. There's nothing tastier! If this is impossible, store freshly-picked peas in a closed plastic bag in the refrigerator for up to four days and they'll still be good. If you planted regular garden peas—the familiar peas in an inedible pod—harvest them when the peas are small inside the pod. If they are overgrown and crammed into the pod, they'll be starchy and less sweet. For the popular sugar snaps that we eat, pod and all, pick them when the peas are still small inside the pods. Again, once the pods are tight with peas, they lose their sweet flavor and are tough and starchy.

We need to remove the stem and strings that are on both sides of the snap pea pod before cooking them. Just grasp the pod right below the stem end and break back the stem. Then pull this stem down the entire pod, pulling the strings on both sides with it. Don't overcook peas. Just a few short minutes either stir fried or steamed and they're ready for the dinner table.

START SEEDS WHILE WAITING FOR SPRING

Cabin fever strikes again! As I gaze out my window at Mother Nature's latest bag of white tricks, I sigh with impatience. What happened to spring? Will my tulips survive this latest siege of cold? What about the poor robins pecking at the frozen ground, searching endlessly for fresh bugs and soft worms? Last week's San Diego trip flashed across my memory: hedges of hybrid tea roses with flowers the size of luncheon plates; blooming birds-of-paradise that appear ready to take off in flight. California sure is lovely this time of year. But back to reality in northern Minnesota. There is a cure for this fever, a recourse that will lift us out of the doldrums and give us a lifeline until spring does indeed arrive. It's called seed starting.

Seed starting indoors isn't for everyone. If you're planning a two-week vacation with friends in Florida during May, forget it! Little seedlings will be long gone by the time you and your tan return to Minnesota. Can't stand dirt under your fingernails or a messy place in your house where trays of plants sometimes get tipped over by Fido? Maybe seed starting isn't for you. Don't even THINK about it if you haven't several large south-facing windows. A big bay window or sliding glass doors are good. Small windows on the north and east will make it downright impossible. Of course you can always invest in lights. I use several rows of flourescent shop lights, plugged into a timer, and have been successful starting seeds for years. These lights are inexpensive to buy and to operate. For 16 hours a day they shine directly above the seedlings, providing them with enough light until they can be set outdoors. One "warm" bulb and one "cool" bulb in each fixture give the entire spectrum of light the plants need.

On the other hand, DO consider seed starting indoors if you want to save some money, try some unusual varieties or make certain your plants are chemical-free. I start seeds because I think it's fun to be a part of the whole growing process. I feel like a real farmer when I watch seeds germinate and gently nurture them along until it's time to set them out in my garden. The satisfaction that comes from watching healthy plants mature under my care is worth the extra mess, fuss and sweeping!

So when do we start? Right now! The rule of thumb is the smaller the seed, the earlier it should be planted. It's already too late for us to start petunias, lavender, snapdragons and many others whose seed is just like dust. These we will have to buy from our trusty local nurseries whose owners spent endless long nights in their greenhouses last February while the rest of us were sleeping soundly in our cozy beds. But there's still time to start tomatoes, peppers, eggplant and even our cold-loving plants like broccoli and cabbage.

Most seed packages will say, "Start indoors eight (or six) weeks before the average date of the last frost in your area". That means the first part of June for those of us up north. The way it feels on this cold day of April, that's not so hard to believe! If you insist on gambling with Mother Nature and intend to set out tomatoes in May just to get that head start on your neighbor, remember that these heat-loving plants will not grow unless the ground is good and warm. Even without an actual frost, they'll just sit tight and wait until everything warms up. Plants that will stand a little frost in the fall can be set out earlier and therefore started earlier. But for our favorite zinnias, marigolds, tomatoes and peppers that have a love affair with the sunshine, we're just in time.

Here are a few ALWAYS and NEVERS for seed starting. ALWAYS label every container so you know what you've planted. Sometimes we can tell which plant is which after it comes up and starts leafing out. But it's about impossible to tell one variety of tomato from another until it starts to bear fruit. NEVER let your seeds dry out. They all need moisture to germinate. After misting the top of the soil right after planting, ALWAYS water the seeds from the bottom. NEVER pour water on top of a flat. Of course this means that each container must have several holes in the bottom for good drainage and watering. ALWAYS use lukewarm water. A splash of ice cold water will make them think winter is back again so they'll stay inside their protective shells.

Once they have sprouted, give your seedlings all the light you can, even if it means hauling them from one window to another. Too little light will mean scrawny, leggy seedlings as they reach for more light from somewhere. If you use grow lights, keep the lights close to the plants and gradually raise them as the plants grow taller. Sixteen (16) hours of light should be alternated with 8 hours of darkness. We humans aren't the only ones that thrive best with 8 hours of sleep! Always start seeds in a commercial starter mix rather than your own garden soil. This way you'll have better luck avoiding diseases that winter over in the soil. The dreaded "damping off" fungus has killed off more seedlings and dashed more hopeful gardeners' plans than stars in the sky. Usually this fungus won't be found in these soilless starter mixes that contain mostly peat and vermiculite.

Spring chores can pile up like ants at a picnic. By doing a little at a time, we can hope to stay ahead of the game. But let's not be over-eager. Those of us who have lived in the northland for awhile know we can't always judge by looking at the calendar. As we wait for spring and planting time, here are some things to keep in mind.

Don't turn over wet soil. Wait until it has partially dried out before bringing the tiller out of the garage. If we work in soil that's too wet, we'll compact it and force out the air that's needed for good plant growth. This usually isn't a problem for me since I garden in sand, but those with clay soils need to be careful about turning it into cement! If you buried your roses for the winter, now's the time to bring them back above ground. If we wait too long to uncover them, the stems often begin to leaf out underground. When we haul them out, this fresh new growth is snapped off. Also, roses left underground tend to mold once the soil starts to warm up. Remove old growth and leaves from perennial gardens but don't move the mulch too far away. Some tender perennials want that protection to shade them from the warm spring sunshine. More damage is done in spring with the freeze/thaw cycle than by the sub-zero temps during winter. As the sun shines on the dark, uncovered soil in our flower gardens, it heats up the surface and encourages the perennial plant just below to awaken and think about popping out. Then zap! comes the cold winter night's chill and sets the poor plant back on its ear. A light covering of straw will keep things stable until spring is here for sure. It could be any day now. I'm ready!

DON'T SPARE THE ASPARAGUS

Planting asparagus is a lot like getting married. There's a sense of commitment. The understanding is that although it's a lot of hard work, the end result will be worth it. And there's the need for endless patience. Plant asparagus and we have to wait three years before we see any on our dinner plates. Plus it needs lots of nourishment and cultivation. Ask any marriage counselor and he/she will say that to make them survive, marriages need lots of nourishing communication and cultivation of good manners and kindness. So it goes with asparagus. Without cultivating, weeds grow up and choke it out. Without fertilizer, asparagus is spindly and tough. Plant an asparagus bed with care and it may last for 25 years or more. Come to think of it, that's longer than most marriages these days!

The first step in planting asparagus is deciding whether or not you like it. We sure do! But it does have a definite character and texture. If you aren't sure if it pleases your family's palate, maybe you'd be better off planting green beans. They're easier and results are a lot quicker! But once you've decided to take the plunge, find a good place to plant. Asparagus needs LOTS of sunshine. It thrives in loose, loamy, sandy soil with plenty of compost, well-rotted manure and peat. Clay soil can be a problem for asparagus unless it's improved with huge amounts of organic matter to help with drainage. Asparagus is tall. Plant it on the north side of your garden so it won't shade other plants.

Now that you've picked the site, grab your spade. Although we don't have to dig clear to China, we will have to dig deep trenches for our plants. While asparagus ferns may reach as high as six feet in the fall, their roots also can be that long once the plant matures. This means we need to loosen the soil underneath and work in lots of good food to supply it for years to come.

A 10-foot-long trench will take about eight asparagus crowns if we space them 18 inches apart. Three of these trenches, or 24 plants, will keep a family of four in plenty of asparagus during its month-long harvesting period, with extra now and then for neighbors.

Dig the trenches deeply, at least a foot and a half. Trenches should be a foot wide, and if you're digging more than one, at least three feet apart. Add five pounds of 5-10-10 fertilizer per 100 square feet and dig in at least a 6-inch layer of manure, compost and peat moss. Work all of this in to a depth of at least 12 inches. The soil should end up being loose and soft, and rich in organic matter.

Now we're ready to plant. Asparagus rhizomes with the growth buds pointing up and roots growing down are available in the spring at local garden centers. Most of these "crowns" will be at least year-old rhizomes. By this time our trench should have at least 6 to 8 inches of space left to be filled. Make small mounds at 18-inch intervals. Set an asparagus crown on top of each mound, spreading the roots down and covering the mound. Cover the crown with 2 to 3 inches of soil. Remember that we want that crown to be at least 4 inches below the soil line once the trench is completely filled in. As the new shoots come up, gradually fill in the trench. By early summer, it should be all filled in and level with the nearby garden. Apply a high nitrogen fertilizer twice a year, in spring at about garden cultivation time, and in early summer after the shoots have appeared. In the case of older, established plants, this would be right after harvest. Asparagus has a hearty appetite, so in the late fall, cover the trenches with lots of old manure. This feeding will keep the plants happy and also protect them from a hard freeze. This is especially important if we have a winter without snow cover.

Now comes the waiting game. Resist the temptation to pick any asparagus for the first two years. The roots are getting established during this time and they need all the food that the spears provide. The third year we can harvest lightly, picking some for meals but leaving other spears to supply root growth. By the fourth spring the plants should be in full gear and ready to do their thing. You might even have extra for the freezer.

Just three little words about weeds in asparagus beds: keep them out! Easier said than done, I know. If we plant those crowns deeply enough, we can carefully cultivate over the top of the trenches in early spring, 2 to 3 weeks before we expect shoots to appear. Mulching is also the key to keeping weeds down. I know a gardener who mulches with grass clippings since they are weed-free. Then there's the farmer-gardener who fenced in her asparagus plot and put her chickens inside. They ate up all the weeds and had the asparagus beetles for snacks. This might work if you have chickens. I have dogs. They're no help whatsoever.

Once you're harvesting asparagus like gangbusters, go out every day and keep those delectable stalks picked. Letting them grow up into lacy foliage will signal the plant to stop producing. As a rule, the harvest season lasts 4 to 6 weeks. After that, smaller shoots will come up and turn to foliage. Leave this foliage and don't take it down until the following spring. It does two things: provides food for the roots and collects snow for cover. I also use small bits of it in with my fresh flower bouquets during the summer.

We were pleasantly surprised to find a small asparagus bed on our property when we first moved back to the North Country. It provided us with many meals until one cold winter without snow cover killed it off. Two years ago I replanted and now we're playing the waiting game until it matures. Until then, maybe Mom and I will take a springtime drive through the countryside back by our old farm and harvest from the road ditches. Through the years, birds have spread the red asparagus berries all throughout the area. The trick is finding the crop before anyone else spots it!

SPRING IS STRAWBERRY PLANTING TIME

If you were to choose your favorite summer berry, which would it be? Many of us can narrow the choice down to three in a hurry: blueberries, raspberries and strawberries. Many other berries also come to mind including lingonberry, blackberry, gooseberry and elderberry, but these first three are the most popular in our part of the world. If pushed to select from these three tasty morsels, I'll guess that the strawberry comes out the winner. In fact, I'll bet my hat on it! Maybe it's because they are the first berries of the season around here. Or perhaps they are so favored because the season is so short and in the blink of an eye they are gone, only to be replaced by the hard California rocks that are labeled "strawberries." We who have tasted the home-grown varieties know better! There's nothing like the sweet, juicy taste of a fresh strawberry to bring us immediately into summer. How do you prefer to eat them? On your cornflakes each morning? Or maybe as a mashed, syrupy concoction drizzled over shortcake. Heaps of fresh berries in a crust covered with a glaze and topped with whipped cream has my taste buds practically dancing in my mouth. Strawberry season can't get here soon enough!

My appreciation of strawberries has, up to this point, been limited to going each June to a you-pick-'em place. Rather than going to the work of raising my own, I leave that struggle up to our local growers. We are lucky to have several in the area that grow wonderful berries! But if you look forward to a challenge and the satisfaction that comes from walking barefoot to the garden early in the morning to pluck a few ripe berries for your breakfast cereal, then strawberry-growing is up your alley. One of the main reasons we gardeners grow our own food is not only the satisfaction of providing for ourselves, but also gaining the knowledge of the fertilizers, pesticides and irrigation methods used to produce this great-tasting food. I shudder to think of the contamination that so easily might come from strawberries grown in other countries where restrictions are fewer than in the States. Strawberries, with their soft, porous exteriors are difficult to wash, ship and store. Any contaminants will quickly be absorbed. When we grow our own, at least we know what, if anything, was used to ward off weeds and bugs.

On the downside, strawberries are a lot of work. A pain in the neck, actually! The fancy lingo is "labor intensive," but no matter which way it's spoken, strawberries are no piece of cake to raise! This must be the reason I've resisted the urge to include some in my limited garden space. Be prepared to put in some extra energy in order to reap the succulent harvest.

Spring is the time to plant strawberries. Any day now they'll be appearing at our favorite nurseries and garden centers. Before we stick them in the ground, there are considerations to keep in mind. First of all, do you have a site ready for them? Strawberries need at least 6 hours of sunlight to be productive and disease-free. They like well-drained fertile soil with a pH around 6, which is about the middle of the acid/alkaline scale. Sandy loam with organic matter worked in for added nutrients is good. An application of commercial fertilizer before planting is advised too. Avoid planting berries in any low-lying area which will be more likely to freeze out in late summer. A site that gets good snow cover is also a positive.

The biggest nemesis of strawberries is weeds, so do your best to make the bed weed-free, especially of quack. Yes, I know this is asking for the moon, but don't say I didn't warn you! Here's where mulch that will help keep down weeds comes in. The most widely used mulch for strawberries is STRAW! Isn't that a surprise! Mulch does double duty. It helps control weeds and also, once the fruit sets, keeps the fruit off the wet ground which helps stop mold and mildew from reaching the berries.

Strawberries do well in raised beds. The ground warms up quickly in the spring, and the berries/plants can be protected from sneaky bandits that also have a taste for these marvelous treats. Of course I'm referring to the birds, chipmunks, squirrels and raccoons, all of which devise elaborate plans to share in our harvest.

Another consideration is the type of strawberries to plant. We have basically three choices: June bearing, ever- bearing and day neutral. Each of these has its pluses and minuses. June bearing strawberries are the traditional berries that ripen at this time of year in most parts of the country. They produce the most fruit, and it usually comes all at one time or within just a couple of weeks. For gardeners who like to freeze/can, this is a good quality. They usually don't flower/set fruit the first year, but set buds in the fall which need to survive the winter. You can see that winter mulching is really important for June bearing types. If they do flower the first year, these flowers need to be removed so that the plant will develop and grow vigorously. Honeyoye and Winona (from the U of M breeding program) are good choices. Everbearing usually produce twice during the season, in the early summer and again in the early fall. They will flower and fruit the first year. Two reliable varieties are Ogallala and Fort Laramie. Day neutrals are the most recent to be available to gardeners. They ripen all summer long. Although the crop is small at any given time, they produce an ongoing harvest until frost when the plants go dormant. Day neutrals are not without their problems. They need additional nitrogen all summer long as opposed to the one dose given to other types. Also, because they fruit/flower all summer, we need to be on guard all the time for the tarnished plant bug that injects a toxin while feeding on the berry. This causes the berries to become gnarled, hard and green with seedy areas, often referred to as "nubbins." The tarnished plant bug is by far one of the most harmful pests and gardeners may need to spray frequently to keep them under control. Two day neutral varieties are Tribute and Tristar.

How soon can we expect berries for our table? Patience! June bearing plants may send out flower stems the first year, but we need to remove them all. This strengthens the plant so it sends all of its energy to the roots and new runners. As for everbearing and day neutrals, remove all flowers up until the first part of July. Wow! Talk about a test of our will power! Just when our mouths are watering for the taste of a berry, we have to pinch off the flower! Keep in mind that by sacrificing the early flowers, the plant will be gaining strength and becoming well-established. This means a better harvest later on. No one ever said delayed gratification was for sissies!

Mulching strawberries, usually done around the plants during the mid-summer, keeps them from drying out, helps stop weed growth, and keeps berries from dragging in the dirt. It also hides slugs. If you have a history of slug problems, mulch will add to that problem. Winter mulch is usually applied after the plants have been zapped with several light frosts that help harden the plants. Once temperatures drop into the mid-twenties, it's time to give them some protection. Mulching protects the fruit buds and stops the freeze/thaw cycle in the early spring. Give the entire area 3 to 4 inches of clean straw. Watch carefully in the spring, as mulch removal can be tricky. Just when to take it off can keep us up nights! A light covering of mulch will be enough to protect plants until the temps stabilize.

Day neutral plants usually last three years. Then it's time to set out new plants. Since they send out few if any runners, we'll have to buy new plants. June bearers need to be restored each summer after harvest. There are a couple of ways to do this. One is to rototill each row leaving a narrow band of plants in our gardens. Reapply fertilizer at this time. Another way is to use our lawn mowers and mow the in about 12 inches wide. Remove any diseased or weak plants. Only the strong, young ones should be left in our gardens. Reapply fertilizer at this time. Another way is to use our lawn mowers and mow the tops of the plants off, collecting the old foliage and getting rid of it. Then till between the rows. Mulch between rows after tilling to control weeds.

It's important to get good planting stock. This usually means buying from a local nursery. Plants that are shipped in from long distances might not arrive in the best condition. Never let the plants dry out. Soaking roots before planting plumps them up and helps keep the plant from wilting. If you're getting plants from an old patch, transplant only the most vigorous looking young plants. Strip off the dead leaves before planting and trim the roots back to about 5 inches. Set the plants with the crown flush with the soil surface or even slightly above. Take care not to plant them too deeply. Give plants a good drink right after planting.

As to spacing, there's some variation depending on the type of berries. June bearing are usually grown in rows with plants 2 feet apart, rows 4 feet apart. Runners from these plants will root during the summer to form a mat of plants 2 feet wide. Everbearing and day neutrals can be closer together since runners aren't allowed to grow. Eighteen inches between plants is adequate.

Strawberries like a lot of water. Until they're well established, water them thoroughly at least once a week. A soaker hose or trickle irrigation is ideal because it doesn't wet the leaves and encourage fungus diseases. Roots are shallow and will dry out quickly in a dry spell. As mentioned earlier, we need to apply fertilizer before planting and once again during the first summer of growth. Day neutrals need to be fertilized more often during the second and third years when they are producing more berries (the first year they don't require constant fertilization as they're only allowed to blossom/fruit later in the season). Slow-release fertilizers are the best to use because they allow a constant supply of nutrients. In any case, don't apply nitrogen late in the summer as this will cause the plants to shoot out a lot of new growth which will likely be damaged by a harsh winter.

After thinking of strawberries for several days this week, I'm getting in the mood to reconsider. Maybe I'll try these day neutrals in one of my raised beds. It's always fun to experiment with something new each year, and a handful of berries would sure taste good on my early morning Cheerios!

YOU SAY PO-TAY-TO AND I SAY PO-TAH-TO

Spuds. Tubers. Taters. No matter what we call them, potatoes are one of the basic food groups here in Scandinavian country. I can't remember a day that passed by on our farm that we didn't sit down to at least one meal with potatoes. Boiled for dinner, fried for supper. Boiled for dinner, creamed for supper. We kids liked them 'scalped'. We ate them because Mom, and every other farmer's wife, grew them in the garden. They were easily accessible and cheap. And, as my mom still insists, they're healthful! She's quite right, as usual! The yummy flavor of small, new red potatoes drenched in browned butter, or smothered in creamed peas is hard to forget There's nothing better! That's why I plant potatoes.

An old wives' tale dictates that we plant potatoes on Good Friday. That plan might have worked this year since Easter was late. But like other plants and seeds, potatoes need some warmth to take off and grow. In our part of the country, we'd likely have to shovel off the snow first before drilling a hole in the ground to plant potatoes so early. May is really a good time to plant potatoes. So go off to the local nursery for some certified seed potatoes and find your spade. Potatoes like either acidic soil or very alkaline soil. Most of us are in luck here as our soil around Bemidji is often acidic (which accounts for the wild blueberries that flourish in the woods). Potatoes thrive in sandy soils that allow for good drainage and potatoes that are nicely shaped. Heavier soils need to have a large amount of organic matter worked in before planting potatoes. I add aged manure and compost to my garden and lightly sprinkle some 5-10-10 fertilizer onto the surface of the soil and till it in. Then I'm ready to plant.

If our seed potatoes are small we can plant the entire thing. Otherwise we'll have to cut the potatoes into quarters, making sure each piece has at least a couple of eyes that will sprout. Let these pieces cure for several days on the kitchen counter or any other dry, open surface before putting them in the ground.

Planting potatoes is a lark. Mark your row with string. Then shove the tip of your spade into the ground along the string, push the handle forward which will make a ditch along the back of the spade, toss in a potato, carefully pull the spade out of the ground and tamp down the soil. Each potato should then be covered with at least 2 inches of soil. Plant potatoes at least a foot apart in rows that are 2 feet apart. Green leaves should poke above ground in a couple of weeks unless we get another cold spell.

Mulch around potato plants with old leaves, hay or straw when they are several inches high to keep in moisture, hold down weeds and keep the sun off any spuds that may work their way to the soil surface. Light on potatoes produces a poison called solanine which causes a green appearance, so it's important that we keep our potatoes covered with soil or mulch. A heavy mulch will also hinder the adult potato beetles that are sleeping in the soil from coming up to lay eggs on the leaves.

This Colorado potato beetle is one of the worst pests to attack our potato crop. Too bad it didn't stay in the Rocky Mountain area where it's native! It's easy to recognize this handsome (let's face it—it IS attractive for a bug!) beetle with its yellow and black rotund back and orange head with black spots. The adult beetles winter in the soil and crawl out as the young plants are developing in early June. They lay yellowish eggs underneath the leaves. Larvae hatch in about a week and have a dandy time feeding on the leaves for a few weeks. Then they go underground and emerge as adults a week later. With both the larvae and adults chomping away on the leaves, they can defoliate plants in no time flat.

20

There are several things we can do if we're invaded by this beetle. Send the kids out to pick them off by hand if there aren't too many of them. A spring tilling of the soil helps as it uncovers the adults that have been snoozing and turns them into bird food. Some gardeners have luck planting garlic and catnip around their potatoes. Apparently the beetles don't like the smell of these herbs. If none of these choices suits you, you can also consider applying a new form of Bt (Bacillus thuringiensis) known as the San Diego strain. This will control the larvae but not the adult beetles.

The best way to keep down potato diseases, and there are many, is to use certified seed potatoes and plant them in a new area of your garden each year. I realize that this is next to impossible for those of us who garden in small spaces, but it's a good plan if you have the room. Potato scab is caused by soils that are too neutral in pH. If the soil is acid (below a pH of 5) or alkaline (above a pH of 7.5), then potatoes are fine. Otherwise they'll get scab. A soil test will determine the pH of your soil.

Potatoes are ready for harvest after the vines have died down. I don't wait for this to happen, because it's the small, new potatoes I'm after! These little spuds are sometimes close to the surface, and if I'm careful I can dig through the soil with my hands and get enough for a meal without tearing out the entire plant. Use a gentle hand on your spade when digging up spuds in the fall. If we damage any—a bruise here, a big gash there—we should eat those for supper and not plan to store them as they'll likely spoil. Not all potatoes flower so don't wait for that as an indication that potatoes are formed.

TREES ARE OUR FOREVER FRIENDS

Arbor Day just slipped by us last week. J. Sterling Morton, a Nebraska newspaper editor, launched what has become a world-wide celebration while encouraging Nebraska folks to plant a tree on the prairie. That was well over a century ago, and we're still following his example today. A tree planted in spring has several months to establish itself before our harsh winter arrives. We also have more energy to dig the hole in the spring, after spending wintry days resting in our recliners. Spring weather pops us out of a relaxing position and has us reaching for our spade before we know what hit us!

Trees are our friends for many reasons. They are the backbone of any landscape plan, offering summer shade and winter windbreaks. The end result is more comfort and less cost when the heating (cooling) bill arrives. They also provide habitat for wildlife, an important concern for us North Country folks. Trees offer good sources of food and cover for all kinds of animals. Several snowy mornings ago I watched a pair of robins nibbling away on left-over Red Splendor crab apples. I'm sure they would have preferred a juicy beetle, but in the middle of a snowfall beetles are hard to come by. If we plant mountain ash, flowering crabs and highbush cranberries as food sources for our feathered friends, we'll be rewarded with both tree and bird beauty.

It doesn't take too much brain power to realize that trees increase our real estate values. A home surrounded by a grove of tried-and-true trees brings a far higher selling price than one standing vigil by itself without a green leaf in sight.

With all these reasons in mind—ornamentation, protection, increased value, link to the future generations, erosion control, habitat for critters—it's no wonder that Minnesotans rank high on the list of prolific tree planters.

Before we reach for the spade or rush off to the garden center, let's consider these questions.

1) Will the species we have in mind survive our harsh winters and thrive in the soil conditions of our yard? EXOTIC doesn't usually carry much weight around here. Although there are continually new varieties available to us each year, not all are hardy in Zones 2 and 3. Remember to check the hardiness recommendation before handing over your money.

2) Is the species relatively pest free? For example, some flowering crabs are more disease resistant than others. Red Splendor (pink)—check them out along the cemetery across from Bemidji State University campus this spring—Donald Wyman (pink to white), and Spring Snow (white) are highly recommended as being disease-free flowering crabs.

3) Is the tree messy, likely to drop seed pods, fruit and broken branches in traffic areas or on your deck? The silver maple is a fast grower, but its brittle twigs break off easily in winds, which can be a nuisance when lawn mowing time comes around.

4) Is the variety the right size for the setting? A tree will grow! As it matures, will it outgrow the place you've planned for it? Trees can encroach on patios and windows, sidewalks and roads. They start out small, just like that wee puppy we couldn't resist, and like the cute pup that becomes a large dog with big dirty feet, we now have an overgrown tree that needs to be trimmed or maybe even removed. The solution? A low-growing relative! Instead of a tall Norway maple which can reach at least 50 feet, choose an Amur maple that stays around 20. Plan for the site available. If you don't have the space on your lot

for a linden, and need a pool of shade on a patio exposed to summer afternoon sun, consider a medium sized tree or a group of smaller trees such as flowering crabs.

5) Do you want fast-growing or will you settle for a slow grower? North Dakota Horticulturist Dave DeCock uses this analogy: Remember that trees are like football players. The big sturdy ones are slow while the fast ones tend to be easier to knock over! Slow growers, because they must be nurtured longer before salable size, are more expensive than fast growers, and once planted, take longer to reach maturity. They are viewed as a long-range investment, a heritage for our children and grandchildren. Their dense wood makes them resistant to breakage in the wind and ice storms. Fast growers, on the other hand, don't have time to develop such strong fibers and are more brittle. Think about it. After a blustery winter, we always find more broken branches beneath a willow than an oak. Fast growers are less expensive, put on a show sooner, and are often graceful additions as shade trees. A combination of several kinds of trees—both slow and fast growing—is the best plan.

Trees are sold in three forms: bare root, container grown, and balled and burlaped. If possible, I recommend bare root because they're the least expensive and the easiest for us homeowners to plant ourselves. They must be planted while they're still dormant—that is, before leafing out—which means early spring planting time. Many fruit trees are available as bare root stock this time of year. Mail order companies ship all of their trees in this fashion.

An advantage of buying a container grown tree is that the roots are in no danger of drying out. The roots of bare root stock must never be allowed to dry out, not even for a few minutes. If we can't plant them as soon as we bring them home, we need to keep them in a cool, shady spot such as a garage or on the north side of our house, and the roots must be covered with a damp mulch or burlap.

Container stock isn't so picky. It comes in various sizes, anywhere from 1 to 15-gallon containers for large trees. Keep in mind that it takes 2 strong men with strong backs and a truck to load and plant a tree from a 15-gallon container. I have the truck but not the men, so I stick to the bare root and small container stuff! Container stock can be planted almost any time during the growing season and is more expensive than bare root because of the extra care and labor necessary.

Balled and burlaped trees are generally those dug from a nursery field with roots and soil tightly wrapped in burlap. A large tree can be safely moved this way, but again, this will take a Paul Bunyanesque person to move it around. B-and-B stock is best planted by nursery folks who have the know-how and the right equipment.

When it comes to planting, keep these points in mind. Don't dig your way to China! In fact, the main reason for the death of newly planted trees is that we plant them too deeply. Plant them only as deep as they were in the field/container. This line should be visible on the trunk of the tree. Dig a hole only slightly deeper than necessary to allow the roots some depth. Backfill in some topsoil from the hole you just dug. If you really want to dig, dig WIDE. That's where the tree roots want to go. Most feeder roots of trees are relatively close to the surface and spread out, not down. The second thing is to water it in well. Using a root stimulant available at garden centers isn't a bad idea. For one thing, it makes us water the tree! Then continue to give it water on a weekly basis, especially if the spring is a dry one. Lastly, don't let grass and weeds surround it. Use a few inches of mulch (wood chips are nice) in a large circle around the tree. Be sure the mulch doesn't come right up to the trunk (leave at least two inches of space) since mulch often becomes the home for mice and voles that cause winter damage. Mulch won't stop moisture and oxygen from reaching the roots, but it will keep the sun out, which discourages weeds.

A TISKET A TASKET, FILL A LOVELY BASKET

I'm a real basket case this time of year! With trowel in hand and dirt under my fingernails, I'm making planting holes in baskets for all sorts of flowers that will hang from our porch and deck railings. Now that the weather has finally warmed up, there's not a moment to waste as we gardeners scurry about on our hanging spree.

Almost everyone has room someplace for a basket of flowers. We can move these hanging baskets around to brighten up any corner, inside or out. As long as it has good drainage and will hold soil, any container will qualify as a hanging basket. I look for containers that are light-weight so they aren't so heavy to move around for watering. Pots that are at least 10 inches in diameter are large enough to hold growing medium so I'm not having to water every time I turn around. Clay pots are my favorite containers for plants that sit on the deck and along the front sidewalk, but they're too heavy to hang. Plastic and wire baskets work the best.

All containers need good drainage. If you have a favorite plastic pot you'd like to convert to a hanging basket, puncture the bottom with at least 5 half-inch diameter holes. An electric drill comes in handy for this task, but a hammer and big nail will do just fine. Cover these drainage holes with a coffee filter before adding planting medium. The filter will let excess water drain out but keep the soil in. A layer of pebbles or broken clay pieces will make the pot too heavy for hanging.

Fill a large pail with water, add bleach (about 1 part bleach to 10 parts water) and find your scrub brush, because you'll want to give your pots a good cleaning before adding soil and seedlings. Bleach will kill off any disease organisms that may be lurking around. Plan to hang your basket in a spot that's safe for the plant and free from human interference. I recall one of my first experiences with hanging planters 20 some years ago when we were apartment dwellers. I thought I was pretty smart, hanging this graniteware bowl full of petunias from the balcony above us. And every time Brian would go outside on the deck to grill burgers, he'd hit his head on the bowl! I found a new spot for that basket in a hurry. Baskets and container plantings require lots of watering, so keep these pots accessible to your watering can or hose.

Choosing plants for our hanging baskets is the most fun of all. We have many choices awaiting us at the local greenhouses. The most important decision to consider is light source. Will your basket be in the sun or the shade? Even though many plants are suitable to basket-growing, some that are much taller than a foot at maturity may look downright silly in a basket. If you plan to combine plants in a single container, remember that their needs must be similar, all shade plants or all sun-lovers, but not a combination of the two. Trailing plants such as black-eyed Susan vine and sweet potato vine are especially suited for hanging baskets. I like to use a combination of trailing and upright plants in the same basket. Overcrowding plants isn't necessary. In fact, while we may want our baskets to look full and gorgeous instantly, giving each plant a little breathing room will allow it to show off, and in the end, it will bush out and grow to fill the extra space.

We may be tempted to fill all our baskets with flowers, but consider a basket of herbs to hang by the sunny back door where we can quickly snip off a leaf or two for a salad or stew. The closer herbs are to our kitchen, the more we'll use them.

I'm still undecided about what makes the best planting medium for containers. For the past couple of years I've used the "soilless" planting mixes. These sterile mixes are part organic materials (usually peat but also can be sawdust, shavings, bark, etc.) and minerals (vermiculite or perlite are usually the materials used) but not actually dirt. These mixes are terrific for starting seeds and transplanting seedlings, but I found that they dried out too quickly as container medium and didn't provide any nutrients. This season I'm experimenting with my own mix of a third of each: topsoil, peat and vermiculite/perlite combination. The vermiculite/perlite will retain water within the granules and the peat is good for both drainage and water retention. There never seems to be a simple answer as to which planting medium is best, but since gardening is more of an art than an exact science, I think this combination is worth a try. There are other commercial potting soils available that have merit. Many contain slow-release fertilizers which will feed the plants throughout the growing season. These soils are usually light-weight but not necessarily light on the budget!

Basket/container plant care is more demanding in some ways than garden plot planting. We need to check the soil moisture often in containers by sticking a finger into the top inch of soil. A dry finger means it's time to water. Soak the plant thoroughly until the water pours out the drainage holes. Water in the mornings so the plant foliage dries out before evening. Container/basket plants need fertilizer on a regular basis because the frequent watering tends to leach out nutrients quickly. I use water-soluble fertilizer (such as MiracleGro) mixed half strength at least once a week.

Some of my favorites for hanging baskets in shady spots are tuberous begonias, impatiens, lobelia, fuchsias and ivies, especially Kenilworth ivy. Mandevilla, bridal veil, thunbergia (black-eyed Susan vine), alyssum and ivy geraniums are wonderful for sunshine. I listed lobelia under the "shady" section although it truly flourishes in the morning sun. Left to fry in the heat of the afternoon sun, it often dries to a frazzle. The All-America winner of 1995, the petunia Purple Wave, turned out to be a terrific container plant and every year since then at least one new Wave or Wave-relative appears on the market. Tidal Wave has a silvery cast and is lovely with other blue flowers. Pink Wave is sensational and remains a favorite. The Waves deadhead themselves which means a lot less work for us gardeners. They need lots of space and water. Only one per basket is really all that's necessary but many folks put in two or three for quicker fullness.

Impatiens are one of the few annual container/bedding plants that not only tolerate but actually flourish in full shade. They are resistant to most diseases and don't appeal to insects, but demand lots of water. Buy small seedlings with deep green leaves. If seedlings have gotten leggy and tall, clip off the top 1/4 of the plant with a pair of shears immediately after you plant them. The New Guinea impatiens are excellent container and basket plants. These impatiens have interesting foliage with various colors, streaks and tints. Remember that New Guinea impatiens, unlike their shade-loving cousins, require partial sunlight for healthy growth. Morning sun is perfect. If they receive hot afternoon sun, they will require constant watering. I'm thrilled with the newer varieties of New Guineas that have the huge 2 to 3 inch blossoms. Like the Wave petunias, all impatiens are self-deadheading. How could we be so lucky?

TAKING THE TOMATO CHALLENGE

Most gardeners I know grow tomatoes. We love them! Our taste buds go crazy whenever we think about the luscious ripe fruits that come from our homegrown tomato vines. It's too bad they're not easier to grow—like lettuce, beans and broccoli. Tomatoes can give us lots of headaches, and I'm not referring to a tomato allergy. I'm talking about the challenge in growing disease-free tomatoes. Last season's wet summer was a nightmare for me and my tomato plants. There wasn't a healthy one in the bunch! This season I'm prepared for an all-out war on tomato pests. You're familiar with the old adage, "An ounce of prevention is worth a pound of cure." Nowhere does it have more meaning than with tomatoes! Here are the steps I'm taking to make sure I have a good tomato harvest this summer.

1. Start out with disease-resistant plant varieties. There are many on the nursery market. Among my favorites are Celebrity and First Lady. Look for the letters VNFTA, which stand for the diseases to which they are resistant. The more letters, the more resistance. Keep in mind that being resistant doesn't mean that a plant will not get disease. It WILL put up one heck of a good fight, though! Heirloom tomatoes aren't resistant at all. They produce the best tasting fruit in the world, if we can get them that far, but they are prone to diseases. Keep a close eye on any heirloom tomatoes in your garden and be prepared to lend a helping hand.

2. Plant tomatoes where they're happiest and that means in lots of sunshine! To stay healthy, tomatoes need a minimum of 6 to 8 hours of direct sunlight daily. Talk about sun-worshippers! They also like to have access to a bit of breeze that will help keep their leaves dry after rains. Herein lies part of my problem. I'm gardening in the trees that surround our home like a fortress. A good stiff breeze rarely reaches my gardens at the center of our yard. After a rainfall it takes hours for my plants to dry off. What's a gardener to do? Provide towels and fans?

3. Give tomatoes plenty of room. They don't take to crowding. It's all about air circulation and keeping those leaves dry. If they're huddled too close together, they'll spread disease in a hurry. A tomato plant needs at least 2-1/2 feet squared in order to get some breeze. If you prune your tomatoes quite severely, they can be spaced closer together.

4. Practice crop rotation if at all possible. Don't plant tomatoes in the same place year after year. Since many diseases come from the soil, it stands to reason that if we can move our plants around from one year to the next, we'll have better luck outwitting the disease. This isn't an easy chore, as many of us are small-time gardeners with space at a premium. Brian built a new raised bed for me this spring which I filled with "good" dirt. It is now home to five caged tomato plants. Will I have better luck in this new spot? That remains to be seen!

5. Mulch underneath your tomato plants with plastic. Having read a recent study that showed that tomatoes like red, I opted for red plastic mulch beneath plants in this new bed. Plastic mulch keeps the soil warm by trapping in the heat. Before covering the entire bed with plastic, I dug the five holes with my trowel so all I had to do once it was covered was make small slits for each plant. The plastic stops the soil from splashing up on the lower leaves during a rain. Later in the summer it's alright to mulch with natural products such as wood shavings, grass clippings and so on, but these mulches have a tendency to keep soil cool. This time of year, tomatoes need to warm up and feel the sun's warmth, so wait until the

plants set fruit before using them.

6. Water from below the tomatoes. This is REALLY important, and something all of us can do. As an experiment, I snaked a soaker hose beneath the plastic mulch. Soaker hoses get only the soil wet, which is a giant step toward keeping tomato plants in good shape. If you don't have one, don't despair. Just lay your regular hose beneath the plants and turn it on to a gentle trickle. Tomatoes need at least 1 inch of water/rain a week in order to grow well. If you must water from overhead, do so early in the morning so the plants have the entire day in which to dry off.

7. Be prepared to spray with a fungicide. This isn't my first choice, but sometimes we have to resort to drastic measures, especially if the weather doesn't cooperate. Cool, wet weather brings out the worst in tomato diseases. If we have any prolonged sieges of this type of weather, I'm planning to spray my plants with a broad spectrum (non-specific) fungicide. If I wait until I see disease, it might already be too late. Bright sunny days with a bit of wind and low humidity are ideal, not only for tomatoes, but for me as well!

8. I almost forgot to mention caging/staking/trellising. All tomatoes except those created especially for patios and small spaces benefit from being caged or staked. Not only do they need the extra support in case of strong winds and rains, but if their leaves are up and off the ground, they'll be less likely to transfer disease from the soil. Determinate or bush tomatoes are in less need of staking than the indeterminate or climbing varieties, but they all need to be kept up and off the ground. This becomes really evident once the heavy fruit starts to form.

Two final words of caution: beware the cutworm and blossom end rot. To prevent cutworms from severing the tender stems of your young seedlings, protect them with a "collar" of heavy paper/cardboard, plastic or a 3-pound coffee tin with the ends removed. Since cutworms live in the top 1 to 2 inches of soil, it's necessary to extend these collars that far down into the ground surrounding our plants. The fruit of tomato plants infected with blossom end rot shows darkened areas at the blossom end. These areas eventually become sunken, black and leathery. Blossom end rot can be prevented by giving plants enough water consistently each week. Don't let tomato plants become totally dried out before giving them a thorough soaking. A good inch every week will keep them growing well. Remember to fertilize every month with a water-soluble fertilizer which is high in phosphorus and lower in nitrogen.

PLAN A CUTTING GARDEN

Summertime means cooking on the grill, fishing and swimming in the nearby lakes, swatting mosquitoes, mowing the lawn once a week and wearing shorts and sandals. Another joy of summer that I impatiently await is having bouquets of freshly cut flowers throughout the house. Ever since my childhood days on the farm, I've been the designated flower arranger. The screen door would slam shut, and off I'd go, scissors in hand, to snip Mom's irises, snapdragons and zinnias which I'd stuff into jars brought up from the basement. This "pick and poke" method wasn't fancy, but we didn't care. Colorful flowers brightened up table tops and dressers in every room of the old farmhouse.

Although summer days haven't arrived, it isn't too early to plan for them. So while husband readies the old fishing boat, I'll decide which flowers to plant so I'll have bouquets here and there until frost. "Cutting flowers" differ from "bedding flowers" in the length of the flower stem. Most bedding flowers that border our gardens have a bushy growth with flowers in clusters on short stems. Popular bedding flowers that we all use are impatiens, alyssum, moss roses and ageratum. They aren't easy to use in bouquets due to their short, weak stems. Cutting flowers, on the other hand, have long, stiff stems that often carry only one flower.

Good cutting flowers can be either perennials or annuals. Most of us gardeners have a combination of both in order to have flowers all summer long. Perennials are the mainstay of our flower gardens, but their bloom time is often quite short. We need perky annuals for continuous bloom and variety.

In addition to having long stems, there are other flower qualities to consider for cut flowers. They often say that variety is the spice of life. This is true when it comes to flowers for bouquets. We want to plant flowers with different forms, tall spikes for height and lines in our arrangements, large round flowers for focal points, and smaller flowers for filler. We'll also need many colors from which to choose. Every good arrangement needs three colors of flowers to make it most pleasing to the eye. This takes some experimentation on our part when it comes to arranging, but we can fuss with that once the flowers are blooming. What we need to do now is plan for many colorful plants so we'll have enough available to make a good selection.

Some flowers naturally have a longer vase life than others. We can do something about this by preparing them correctly when we pick them, but sometimes there's not much we can do with certain flowers that droop and drop petals quickly. I also like to think of fragrance when planting flowers for cutting. What a joy it is to stick one's nose into a nearby bouquet and take a deep whiff! Some flowers are definitely more fragrant than others, so keep this in mind.

Some of my favorite perennials for cut flowers are peonies, roses (hybrid teas are best), lilies, mums, yarrows and daisies as focal flowers; and delphinium, astilbe, liatris, coral bells, sedum and globe thistle for lines and fillers. Perennials usually need at least a year in the garden before they'll bloom, so if you plant them this spring, don't count on cutting until next year. Hybrid tea roses are an exception.

The list of annuals that make good cut flowers is almost endless. Annuals for height and line are larkspur and snapdragons. Bells of Ireland, which are excellent for dried arrangements, are also good cut flowers. Their solid green color and cup-shaped flowers make them an unusual addition to a bouquet. But watch out for their prickly stems. Many annuals are good form flowers. Asters, cosmos, zinnias, annual chrysanthemums, marigold, dahlias and glads come to mind right away. Petunias are used often because they're so colorful and many of us gardeners have them growing all over. They won't last long in bouquets and are considered tops as bedding flowers. Lisianthus and lavatera are two less common annuals, but they're definitely worth planting. Both hold their blooms for a long time indoors and are absolutely lovely. Sweet peas and bachelor buttons are smaller and can be used as focal points but they make better filler flowers. Sweet peas can't be beat when it comes to fragrance. One small bouquet will perfume an entire room! Other good fillers are statice, salvias (I'm especially delighted with the blue Victoria salvia), and celosias.

As for greens in our bouquets, there's none better in my opinion than asparagus fern, which grows beautifully in hanging baskets. Spikes (dracaena) that we often include with geraniums are great for adding height. Iris and glad leaves work well for this, too. Grasses, even after they have seeded out, add interesting color and sense of motion to bouquets. Peony and lupine leaves stay lovely long into the summer and add green fullness when fewer flowers are available.

Just for something different, think about adding herbs to your bouquets. Not only do they add unusual textures but they also give off aromas that will tickle your nose and add a surprise. Parsley looks as good in a bouquet of flowers as it does decorating our dinner plates. As an annual, it's easy to grow and is a great companion to a pot of red geraniums. Basil, also an annual, adds color and texture to bouquets. I'm thinking foremost of purple ruffles basil that I've started in a flat in my basement. Have you ever thought of using dill for bouquets? Larger heads of fresh dill make great form flowers while the smaller heads are good fillers. Sage is a hardy perennial with a unique gray-green color and a fuzzy texture. Artemisia also has a grayish cast. The variety Silver King has longer stems which makes it good for bouquets. Use your imagination. Keep your eyes open for textures, unusual colors and unique shapes of leaves.

To keep all of our flowers blooming longer and more luxuriantly, snip off all old blooms, fertilize at least once a month with water soluble fertilizer, and water deeply and often during dry spells. Now is the time to work a granular fertilizer (10-10-10 is good) into the ground surrounding our perennials. Be careful not to damage any emerging shoots. Snatch weeds out of your flower patch with a determined hand, and make daily trips to your flower gardens to keep an eye on things. Flowers are most lovely by mid-morning while they're still fresh with dew and not yet wide-eyed from hot sunshine. Enjoy them at their peak performance and give them encouragement and praise. I sing to my plants. My neighbors might not think it's such a good idea, but once in a while I catch flower heads nodding along. Have I been out in the sun too long?

CAPTURE IT IN CONTAINERS

Anyone can be a gardener. All it takes is a bit of patience, a sense of adventure, a fearless attitude toward bugs and dirt under fingernails, and a pair of old jeans or overalls. (A straw hat comes in handy, too!) Container gardening makes it possible by eliminating some of the heavy work. There's no tilling or heavy digging. By bringing plants to within easier reach, container gardening is easier on our sore backs and stiff knees.

The pluses of container gardening add up to a long list. With containers we can create gardens where plants normally don't grow—on patios and decks, apartment balconies and window sills, front stoops and back doors where friends come to call. We can move containers of colorful plants so we can see and smell them often during the day and maybe pull a weed or two. We can group flowers together for a bright splash of color in the corner of our deck where we can sniff their fragrance and watch as hummingbirds flit from one to another. Or we can bring some pots indoors for a few hours if we're having dinner company and want some fresh plants inside the front door to perk up the entrance.

There are a few drawbacks to keep in mind before heading off to the nursery. First of all, container plants dry out quicker than those growing in our gardens. They need a constant supply of water, at least once a day in the middle of summer. If we're having a lengthy vacation and can't count on our next door neighbor to watch over our plants, we may need to reconsider this idea. Too bad there isn't a kennel for container plants!

Secondly, container gardening isn't for cheapskates! There's the initial cost of buying containers (more about this later) and then the growing medium. Container plants need more added fertilizers than garden plants, so this adds to the cost.

What makes a good container? Look for one that's suited for the area where you'll use it. Plastic pails are fine for hidden corners in the back yard, but you probably won't want something so hideous by your front door! All containers need drainage holes in the bottom and sides near the bottom so that excess water runs out freely. Few plants will survive if they have wet feet for very long. Choose a container that will accommodate the number of plants that will go in it. Common sense tells us that the larger the plant at maturity, the larger the container needed for it. Small, low-growing annuals will survive easily in shallow pots, but taller vegetables and flowers need more root room and also look better in deeper, larger containers.

Look for containers that have wide bases so they won't be easily tipped. Small, light weight pots on balconies may be blown over in a wind. A better choice for these areas are larger pots of heavier materials. Be sure that hooks and supports for hanging baskets and window boxes are secure and strong.

Clay pots are my all-time favorites. These porous pots breathe and have less tendency to stay soggy. In fact, the opposite is often true—they dry out too quickly. But still I prefer them to plastic, both in looks and function. They are a bit heavy and can crack, but they're inexpensive and I like the casual, informal look they give to plants.

Hunting for pots is pure fun! I am always on the lookout at auctions and yard sales. You never know when you'll find the perfect pot. Check in your garage, basement, attic or storage shed. I discovered an old graniteware commode out in the woods by our house last fall. Now that's a REAL pot! Since it's metal and has no drainage, I'll plant in a plastic pot and set it on a few stones inside the commode. A red geranium will call it home this season. My best advice? Be creative.

All plants need water, oxygen, nutrients and something to hold them in place. Container plants are no different. One type of medium available for container plants that will provide all of the above is what we call "soilless" soil. It's not garden dirt, and in fact contains no dirt at all. It's a combination of peat moss, vermiculite, perlite, and sometimes, but not always, fertilizers. These soilless mixes work well because they're lightweight, retain water without becoming soggy, and provide good drainage. They're also free of diseases and insects. Real soil from our gardens is heavy, gets crusty on the top and often contains unwanted critters and weed seeds. The main problem with these soilless mixes is they are costly and usually contain no nutrients, so we need to fertilize right away. If the soil mix has slow-release fertilizer already added, we don't need to add any until seedlings are growing well. Then we will begin fertilizing with a water soluble food such as MiracleGro. During the summer when plants are growing fast and furiously, I fertilize container plants at least once a week. First of all, water the plant well until water flows out the drainage hole. Then come around with the water/fertilizer mix and give the plant a healthy drink. To avoid root burn, I mix this fertilizer at half the dose printed on the box. If it calls for two spoonsfuls per gallon, I'll use only one.

Many annual flowers are perfect for containers. Some of the most popular are petunias, impatiens (my aunt calls them Busy Lizzies), alyssum, geraniums, marigolds, lobelia and begonias. But let's not forget about zinnias, salvia, moss roses, nasturtiums, nicotiana (flowering tobacco), calendula (pot marigold), dianthus and verbena. Consider baskets of herbs or salad greens in a sunny spot by your back door, or large pails of peppers, tomatoes and even summer squash. Fresh green cascades of asparagus ferns, vinca vines and all sorts of ivy mingle with the bright splashes of flowers and are welcome additions to summer bouquets for our kitchen table.

When choosing vegetables, if possible select plants bred specifically for containers. Patio tomatoes are an example. They don't sprawl all over and yet produce good-tasting fruit. Look for smaller sized cukes and melons that make them more adaptable to containers. Grow UP whenever possible. Cukes on a trellis are easy to pick and don't take up so much space. Most vegetables need at least 6 hours of direct sunlight to produce. If they get too much shade they'll still leaf out, but harvest will be sparse indeed.

Check all container plants carefully and often for pests. This is a definite advantage with container gardening because it's much easier to see these unwelcome critters when we can get up close and confrontational! Handpicking often works with bugs if we catch them early. Sharp blasts of water from a hose can take care of aphids, but it doesn't hurt to have a supply of insecticidal soap at the ready in case stronger ammunition is needed.

LILAC LORE

All winter long I dream about lilac blossom time. Lilacs bring back fond memories. I can see it in my mind's eye just as if it were yesterday—the little auditorium perfumed by the huge bouquets of lilacs as the families and friends of the graduating class of 1963 waited impatiently for the procession. There were no florists in that tiny rural town. We relied on Mother Nature to put on her timely show. Then we would search the neighborhoods for the spectacular purple spires that would adorn the auditorium stage.

Last year I decided it was about time that we had some lilacs in our own yard. I planted five small shoots of the hybrid called Sensation that have magenta blooms with white edges. This final week of April the leaf buds are starting to swell. If we get some warm days soon, the leaves will pop into life in a hurry.

Lilacs are one of the hardiest, most versatile shrubs we can plant in our area. We can get them in many shapes, colors and sizes so they will be at home in a hedge, a planting by the foundation of our house, or a specimen planting, beautiful all by itself. Lilacs won't grow down in the South because they need a seasonal resting period (don't we all?). That's winter to us, folks! Southerners have their magnolias and dogwood. We North Country citizens have lilacs and rhubarb!

Autumn is actually the best time to plant lilacs, after the leaves have dropped and before the ground freezes. But if you're eager as I am to have these perfumed beauties in your yard, there's still time this spring to set them out provided we get them in the ground before they have leafed out.

Lilacs like full sun and lots of open air where they can catch a summer breeze. They will grow well in almost all types of soil but they aren't happy in an acidic spot. This could be a problem for us in our area. The best idea is to take a soil sample of your site and send it down to the University. If the pH of your soil is toward the acidic side, you'll want to add a good handful of bonemeal down below the root area and work it into the soil. Bonemeal is a good fertilizer for lilacs, and it contains the lime that can sweeten acid soil. Work in some old manure and compost, and a bit of low nitrogen fertilizer (5-10-5) before setting the lilac in the prepared hole. Good soil preparation will bring out those flowers that we wait all winter to see. Planting instructions usually come with purchased shrubs. As a rule of thumb, plant lilacs at least six feet apart. Lilacs are easy on us. They don't require a lot of fuss and take care of themselves except during a dry spell when we'll need to water everything in sight. Pull out weeds that sneak up around the base of the plant. A 4-inch layer of leaf or straw mulch will help keep down weeds and retain moisture.

We don't need to worry about pruning lilacs for the first 4 to 5 years. Let the plant develop several branches from the base instead of only one or two. Later on we can remove stems that have grown too tall. Once the lilac is thriving we may need to prune out weaker wood from the center of the bush. This is a chore that we'll do as soon as the flowers have dried up. If we wait until late summer or fall to prune, we'll remove flower buds that the plant has already set for next spring. If you have an older bush that's gone crazy with runaway growth, you'll need to prune in stages. Each year for the next three years remove one third of the old stems, cutting them back at the base of the shrub.

As soon as our lilacs are done flowering we need to find our shears and get out there to snip off those old flowers. This helps keep the plant growing vigorously for the rest of the season and means more blooms the following spring.

Bugs usually aren't a problem for lilacs. About the only disease that attacks lilacs is powdery mildew. You'll see the whitish dust on the leaves in late summer, especially if the season has been wet and humid. We can control powdery mildew by dusting with sulfur as soon as we notice it.

There are probably a zillion different varieties of lilacs, but here's a list of several that grow well in our area and can be bought locally. Miss Kim and Dwarf Korean are small shrubs that grow to 5 feet high, perfect for foundation plantings. The Common Purple is the old fashioned favorite that suckers all over the place but is still loved because it's just like the one Grandma had in her backyard. French Hybrid lilacs come in a variety of gorgeous colors and don't send out suckers, but they are slower growing in our area and reach about 10 feet. Canadian lilacs have leathery, elongated leaves, a later bloom time, don't sucker and are extremely hardy.

One more thing. Remember that the secret of staying in the "bloom of youth" is the lilac. Lilac the dickens about your age!

SUNFLOWERS CHEER UP OUR GARDENS

Have you ever seen a field of sunflowers stretching as far as the eye can see? It's a spectacular sight! When late August rolls around, before the frost has had a chance to darken the flowers, I jump in my car and make a southwestern jaunt to see my mom. I roll down the car window, hang my elbow out and take the backroads in search of yellow fields. I'm never disappointed. Many farmers are finding the sunflower crop a money-maker. Instead of continuous fields of oats and barley, acres of yellow sunflowers appear here and there. The sight is enough to make a person smile clear through to the heart! Take a drive through the country in the late summer and you'll see what I mean.

Nothing is easier to grow than sunflowers. After the threat of frost passes by and the ground warms up, they almost spring up from the ground once we plant the large seeds. If we soak the seeds overnight, they'll germinate even faster. Some sunflowers are perennials, but the ones most familiar to us are the annuals. One sure way to get your kids interested in gardening is to give them a packet of sunflower seeds. Little hands are able to handle these large seeds without trouble. The fact that they are up and quickly growing within a few short days makes them an ideal plant for kids, who can lose interest unless there's action in the garden. Plant sunflowers in the full sun, give them plenty of space—12 inches between most plants. Aside from the usual weeding, sunflowers need little care compared to many other annual flowers. They thrive in hot, dry weather conditions and are the perfect flower to use as a backdrop to the rest of our plants.

Sunflowers are an American original. Indians west of the Mississippi were cultivating sunflowers when the explorers from the Old World discovered them several hundred years ago. Indians used sunflowers for their food value, as a dye, and for the fibers from the stalks and roots. We have expanded the uses these days to include everything from snacks to potpourri. Sunflower oil is used for making margarine and cooking oil. We use the flowers for gorgeous arrangements to brighten our homes. Crafters use dried sunflowers in wreaths, scented potpourri and other homespun, country-inspired creations. And of course, sunflowers turn to seeds which are favored by birds, squirrels and many other animals.

One terrific sunflower was even chosen an All American Winner for 2000. It's called "Soraya" and stands out with its 4 to 6-inch blooms of golden orange with chocolate-brown centers. According to the catalog information, they will reach 5 to 6 feet, and branch out with 18-inch stems producing multiple flowers which are excellent for cutting. I can hardly wait to see if it's as spectacular as the reports claim! Another sunflower I'm trying for the first time this year is called "Velvet Queen." This is called a novelty sunflower as it produces dark burgundy-red flowers instead of the usual yellow/gold. The picture on the packet is gorgeous! I hope my results will be the same!

There's a sunflower suited for almost every garden as they are available in a variety of sizes. Not all are the towering 6-foot giants. "Pacino" is a dwarf sunflower, great for pots and fabulous as flower borders. It reaches only 24 inches (slightly shorter if grown in a pot). "Teddy Bear" is another compact version reaching 18 inches with double golden yellow blossoms. Make sure to read the packet information carefully before purchasing your seed so you know exactly what you're getting. With all the different varieties on the market these days, you're sure to find one that fits your garden space.

There's something about sunflowers that makes us all smile. Maybe it's the way they seem to follow the sun with their bright faces. Or maybe it's their bold colors—yellow, orange, even mahogany red—that catch our eye. Whether standing guard at the back of our gardens or nodding from a nearby field, sunflowers warm our hearts.

If you're looking for a good bush to add to your yard, you won't go wrong with the American highbush cranberry. It provides color in all four seasons, plus gives food for the birds as well. In the spring, it produces pretty lace-like clusters of creamy white flowers. By August it's a lush green with bright red berries. Come fall, the leaves turn a vibrant color, and once winter rolls around the berries provide a vivid splash of color until the birds find them! The highbush cranberry belongs to the Viburnum family, which is a large one. When selecting a bush for your backyard, consider the size. Some varieties are smaller and more compact such as Alfredo, which grows only 6 feet high and doesn't sprawl out as much as its relatives. The highbush cranberry is hardy to our area, thrives in sun and partial shade, and needs moist soil with good drainage. No matter where you plant it, as a border or specimen plant it's sure to be a hit.

Some late spring reminders: resist the urge to cut off the faded tulip leaves that look messy. Instead, plant annuals around them and in no time they'll be surrounded by color. Tulip bulbs need the nutrition provided by these leaves in order to bloom again next year. If you work in some granular fertilizer around your perennials (10-10-10 is a common one), be sure no fertilizer touches the plants or they'll get "burned." Stay several inches away from the base of the plants. The time to stake plants that will need support this summer is when you plant them. If we push in stakes later on when the plants are bushy and mature, there's a danger we'll harm the roots.

Summer ❦

Summer ❧

Life takes on a new speed during the summer, almost like shifting from low to high gear in the '49 Chevy that was our first family car on the farm. We knew that the bright, long days of June and July and the intense heat of August were only fleeting moments, leading quickly to autumn. All of our energies went into planting, growing and harvesting during those three short months. Farm living didn't allow for much leisure although we managed to sneak in reading breaks and coffee with neighbors. As I look back in my mind's eye, those days were a blur of activity. From sun-up to sun-down there were always chores that demanded our attention. As a teenager, I was far too glamorous to have to work in Mom's garden, or so I figured. That didn't exclude me, much to my chagrin. Even when on vacation from college, I'd end up podding peas and breaking beans which eventually ended up in the huge freezer in the entry. Riding the lawn mower offered my sister and me a respite from the tedious gardening chores and a chance to enhance our suntans. Summer was a fast-moving time that never lasted as long as we hoped. Once in a while we'd pop corn, load up the car and go to the drive-in movie, or pack a picnic and head for nearby Maple Lake. But for the most part, summer was for working. We could all rest in the winter, but for now, there was work to be done on the farm.

Not a whole lot has changed since then. Summers still go by in a flash and we bustle around like chickens-with-their-heads-cut-off! Once June arrives, North Country gardeners work fast and furiously to get everything planted. It's too chancy to set plants out earlier unless we protect them from frost which can hit anytime up to Memorial Day. With only 90 to 100 growing days, there's no time to waste if we want to see any flowers blooming or vegetables ripening. Summer becomes a blend of watering, weeding, hoeing, mowing, pruning, picking, snipping and cutting. Is it any wonder that unless we keep a log of our weekly activities, we've forgotten them by the following winter? My summer gardening plans have broadened to include taking more photos, watching butterflies, listening to the birds and inviting friends to sit with me on my garden bench to share garden stories. Summer is a treasure. It will be over before we know it. I wonder where I should set my bench this year? If you don't have one, get one! We all need a place to sit and admire our gardening successes.

COTTAGE GARDENS HAVE OLD FASHIONED CHARM

How do you describe a cottage garden? Several words pop into our minds: romantic, welcoming, colorful, informal. I'll add another that appeals to me—fragrant. The term comes from the small garden outside of an English cottager's home where everything grew together cheek by jowl—flowers, vegetables, herbs and fruit. There was no green grassy yard as we know it. Every square foot was planted into something productive.

The American version of a cottage garden today is an informal grouping of a mixture of plants, usually those requiring little care or fuss, that show a medley of colors. We don't even need a cottage! A small plot is ideal for this enchanting type of garden, so don't give up if your space is limited. For a cottage garden look, here are some ideas.

Plant flowers in groups or clumps of at least 3 of a kind. Set plants close enough together so that when they are mature, no soil shows. Here's where underplanting comes in. Stick colorful annuals, even perennials, beneath shrubs for masses of color. Use ground covers beneath and around lilies, clematis and any other perennials that like to have cool feet.

Give flowers a backdrop. We can use shrubs, picket fences or trellises for this easy task. Break up any large, open spaces into smaller "rooms" by using paths, fences or even walls. A cottage garden gives a feeling of intimacy and privacy, a sanctuary where we can hide from the rest of the world. Use vines tumbling down from these walls/fences/trellises, flowering vines such as dropmore honeysuckle vine or virgin's bower (a type of clematis) or jackmani clematis. Think of this garden as a get-away, a mini-vacation without the pressures of travel and lost luggage!

Make sure to include a garden bench or chair tucked into a shady nook where you can sip mint juleps (or iced tea!) and soak in the pleasures of your surrounding plants.

The list of favorite flowers for a cottage garden is long and fascinating. It includes both annuals and perennials plus flowering shrubs. Let's begin with the essentials, flowers that no respectable cottage gardener would leave out.

Hollyhocks. I can't imagine a cottage garden without these old-fashioned favorites. Next to porches, peeking into windows—they never fail to delight the eye! Hollyhocks have been cottage flowers ever since the crusaders brought them back to England after their escapades. Once in America, they spread quickly and are as popular as ever today with us gardeners. I prefer the single flowering types although many prefer the frilly doubles that remind me of silky carnations. Hollyhocks grow luxuriantly in rich soil with plenty of moisture. They need lots of sunshine and may need staking since they sometimes reach 8 to 9 feet. If you're troubled with hollyhock rust, a fungus common to these flowers, treat them early with a fungicide such as Funginex, or dig them up and dispose of them (not in your compost pile please). Don't plant them for a couple of years in that spot, but try again later. Hollyhocks are a biennial that self seed so we often think of them as perennials. Biennials are plants that produce leaves the first year and flowers the second. Then they are finished. Kaput!

Many think of delphiniums as the queens of the cottage garden with their majestic spires of blossoms. They are hardy and will live 3 to 5 years if given plenty of support from wind and rain, and are content with their planting site. Delphiniums grow anywhere from 2 to 6 feet tall depending on the variety. They like moist but well-drained loamy soil and are available in a multitude of lovely colors. Their flowers are either single or double with the outer petals forming a spur while the smaller inner petals cluster around the stamen to form what is called a "bee." Delphiniums need lots of water around flowering time. After flowering, cut back the stem (not the leaves!) to the ground and then fertilize to encourage new shoots.

No cottage garden should be without foxglove. Foxglove (digitalis) has bell shaped spotted flowers on tall spires above clumps of hairy foliage. They grow best in partial shade but will tolerate full sun in cooler zones if given enough moisture. Like delphiniums, foxglove likes moist, well-drained, fertile soil. It isn't always reliable as a perennial in our zone 3 and is actually another biennial that self seeds in milder zones. A new variety called Foxy will bloom the first year, grows to 3 feet and blooms in delicate shades of cream, yellow, rose and white. I planted three "foxies" this week and look forward to their marvelous spires in bouquets as well as gracing my garden.

Native to our country, phlox has been a favorite for ages. Its sweet scent makes it delightful in bouquets as well as in our gardens. There are both annual and perennial phlox. Annuals are shorter but they all are resilient and fragrant. Another fragrant favorite is dianthus, commonly called "pinks." Carnations are members of this family that sports feathered or fringed petals and swollen joints (do they have arthritis, too?) Their delightful clove scent attracts noses as well as bees! Put them in a sunny spot with rich soil and good drainage and cut off faded flowers to prolong bloom. No-old fashioned garden is complete without these nostalgic, scented beauties!

Others to consider: sweet peas, bleeding hearts, lady's mantle, old fashioned shrub roses, lupin, allium, purple coneflower, monk's hood, black-eyed Susans, Queen Anne's lace, cleome, columbine, cosmos, love-lies-bleeding, nasturtium, verbena, veronica and pansies.

Remember that there are no rules to follow about what goes into your cottage garden. Grow the plants that catch your fancy. If you're a fragrant-flower fanatic, indulge this preference. Include a mixture that produces exuberant flowers with pleasing textures and shapes. Think "nostalgia." Do you remember your grandmother's flower garden? That will give you old-fashioned inspiration!

FRAGRANT FLOWERS ATTRACT NOSES AND BEES

What's the first thing you do when someone hands you a rose? You put it up to your nose and take a big whiff, right? You're disappointed if that rose doesn't have a sweet scent. The fragrance of flowers adds so much to their beauty. I recall one early morning last summer when my daily dog walk ended in a stroll around my small flower garden behind the house. As I sniffed the humid air, my nose was greeted by the spicy perfume of dianthus and the sweetness of alyssum. I realized then that I had planted these flowers for the delight they offer my olfactory senses as well as for their visual beauty.

Lilies are some of the most fragrant flowers we can put in our gardens. Last year I planted three Star Gazer lily bulbs that bloomed in August. I could smell their heavy scent from several feet away. Some varieties of lilies are more fragrant than others. Check each variety for hardiness and fragrance before you buy.

My aunt shared several tubers of her pink peonies with me last fall, and although they won't bloom for at least two years, I already anticipate the heavenly fragrance they will lend to springtime. A bunch of peonies set on your dining room table will perfume the house for days if you don't object to an ant or two scurrying around the vase.

Fragrance with spice and everything nice describes the dianthus family of flowers. Pinks, carnations and sweet williams are members of this family. Their vibrant colors and various sizes make them perfect for indoor bouquets. They aren't always hardy for our area, so we need to treat them as annuals. These sun-loving flowers are worth a spot in our gardens and do well in sandy soil.

Hardy phlox, often a mainstay of a perennial flower bed, is loved for its intense colors and pleasant perfume. Phlox is impressive as backdrops for smaller plants and thrives under full sun and moist soil.

Lilies of the valley are so fragrant that a handful of blossoms in a small vase will perfume an entire room. They spread quickly and can be used as a ground cover for shady areas. Candytuft is a semi-hardy perennial with a low growth habit, perfect for rock gardens. It welcomes spring with a cover of small, fragrant white flowers.

Sweet peas, the queen of all fragrant flowers in my book, require a trellis or some other method of support. Sow them early in rich soil as they prefer cool weather. A bouquet of sweet peas will do for a room what no jar of potpourri can do!

Mention sweet smelling flowers and most people immediately think of roses. Not all roses are fragrant. Check the varieties first before you plant. The Hansa shrub rose that Mom and I dug up from the farm has clusters of fragrant deep rose blooms. Blossoms of the shrub roses Bonica and Therese Bugnet are somewhat fragrant also. Magnifica, a hardy rugosa rose, is highly fragrant. If you prefer hybrid tea roses Chrysler Imperial, Double Delight, Mister Lincoln, Fragrant Cloud, and John F. Kennedy are noted for their fragrance.

Lavender is fragrant both fresh and dried. We can use leftover blossoms for potpourri pots, and as sachets tucked in drawers.

We can choose many fragrant annuals for our garden. Years ago the bees and hummingbirds in our backyard were delighted by nicotiana (flowering tobacco). I was surprised by its lovely scent. This spring I started white nicotiana called Fragrant Cloud. It's a slow grower so I'm keeping fingers crossed that it will be ready for the garden by Memorial Day.

Cosmos, a tall, graceful annual is one of my favorites for cutting. Its delicate scent is matched by its lacy foliage and pastel colors of pinks and violets. The ever popular petunia is a favorite bedding flower, loved for its durability, gorgeous colors and sweet scent. Every year I plant several in containers that I keep on the deck by the side door. I like to have them close by so I can savor their sweetness whenever I step outside to check on the dogs. Hummingbirds are crazy about them, as they are about most trumpet-shaped flowers.

Sweet alyssum is always in demand at the garden centers. It makes gorgeous edging for borders and beds and is also good for hanging baskets. Carpet of Snow contrasts beautifully with brilliant petunias, verbena, salvia, and many other bedding flowers. Heliotrope, another aromatic annual, reaches a foot in height and is a vivid violet-blue. Stocks, scabiosa, and four o'clocks are other fragrant annuals to consider.

GLADS MAKE ME HAPPY

I stumbled across them in the basement as I was looking for our rain gauge. There they were, safe and sound in the brown paper bags I put them in late last fall for winter storage. Even though they need almost 3 months to bloom, I'm putting them in the ground and taking a chance. Unless they're planted, they won't live through the season until next summer so there's nothing to lose.

At first glance there's not much room left for these glads in my small flower garden. But on second inspection, I'll sneak some in alongside the tulips that are in various stages of drying. I'll use my narrow trowel in hopes of disturbing the tulips only a little. Glads need lots of sunlight and decent soil. While I'm down in the basement, I'll bring up the package of bone and blood meal to add to the holes that I'll be digging. Some old gardening books used to advise adding bone meal to the soil beneath all bulbs, but bone meal only supplies phosphorus and a bit of calcium. Most plants, even heavily flowering ones, need more of a complete fertilizer now and then. The blood meal is an organic source of nitrogen, so combined with bone meal it's a good provider. There are ready-formulated fertilizers made just for bulbs on the market. These slow-release formulas are often in the 9-9-6 or 5-10-20 proportions. Any of these will be good for bulbs.

Glad flowers come in almost every color we can imagine—green, lavender, salmon, even brown. One of my favorites is the ruffled white with a red throat. According to the May 1990 issue of *Minnesota Horticulturist* magazine, every gladiolus variety is assigned a three-digit classification number. The first digit tells the floret size, the second is the basic color, third is the depth of color. The only number most of us gardeners need to heed is the first number indicating size, as most catalogs and garden centers provide descriptions and even photographs of the glad corms they sell. The small (2 1/2 to 3 1/2) and medium (3 1/2 to 4 1/2) sized cultivars are likely the most suitable to those of us who raise glads for the fun of it and not for competition. The large ones lose the label "easy care" and require more gardening attention.

If possible, don't plant glads in the same location year after year. Fungus problems can sometimes develop in bulbs, and by moving bulbs from one area to another, these diseases are discouraged. For small space gardeners like myself, this crop rotation is next to impossible. I'll just keep an eye out for any glad leaves that are discolored and misshapen and yank them out right away. Most of the glad bulbs available to us are the taller varieties and need to be planted in groups at the back of our gardens. The shorter varieties which are less common need the sunnier spots up front. Keep in mind that glads make a more spectacular showing when we group them together.

Once we've enriched the planting site with aged compost and time-release fertilizer, it's time to set in the corms. Plant large corms 4 to 6 inches deep and about 6 inches apart. Smaller corms can be closer to the soil surface, 3 to 4 inches deep and 4 inches apart. Glads are thirsty characters and need to be watered regularly, at least once a week if rains don't cooperate. Once buds are visible along the stems, it's a good idea to water with half-strength fertilizer for good flower development. Other than providing stakes for the taller varieties, there's not much work involved for us gardeners where glads are concerned. Since some glads will grow to 3 to 4 feet, they welcome any support so they won't be broken off, bent or twisted in a strong wind.

Glad flowers open one at a time from bottom to top and keep on blooming for many days. For this main reason, I find they make terrific cut flowers for bouquets and arrangements. As the bottom flower wilts and hangs its head, snip it off and wait for the others to open up. They're absolutely grand!

From the "tidbits of useless information" department, the name *gladiolus* comes from the Latin *gladius* meaning "sword" which describes its spike-like stem. A sword or two along with a cut glad stem is usually enough for a tall vase, but be sure to leave at least 4to 5 leaves to feed the corm for next year's growth.

Since many of us grow glads for bouquets, it's important to remember that the more foliage we leave on the plant when cutting, the better off the corm beneath the ground will be. As soon as we cut the flower, a new corm begins to grow. If we cut off too much foliage, there won't be enough food made for the corm to develop into its full size. If you leave glads blooming out in your garden, it's a good practice to cut off the old flowers before seed pods form. The plant's energy will then be channeled into developing the corm rather than into making seeds.

In the fall, dig up the corms before a killing frost. Leaves should be yellow or brown by this time. Snap off the old dried-up corms on the bottom and cut the leaves back to 3 inches or so. Wash corms off in running water and air-dry them for several days. When they are completely dry, dust them with Sevin dust to reduce chances of thrips wintering over in the corm. Store corms in open paper bags, old mesh onion bags or nylon stockings—any container that allows for air circulation, but don't store them in plastic bags! Then place them in a dark, cool, dry place that stays as close to 45 degrees as possible. A cold spot in the basement or a tuck-under garage are two good places. Don't let them freeze.

Wire tomato cages make good plant supports for flowers such as dahlias, peonies and sweet peas. The trick is in remembering to cage them BEFORE they get so large that they won't fit in the cage easily. Trust me. I know what I'm talking about! A few days ago I had to surround one of my peony plants with a circular wire support. Had I remembered to do this when the plant was still small, there would have been no problem, no holding of my breath as I cautiously bent the branches to fit within the circles. But it worked and now it's assured of encircling arms just in case the flowers become heavy with dew and rain.

Believe it or not, I even found the rain gauge I was looking for down in the basement. Now I'll know for sure how much moisture Mother Nature sends down without having to ask my neighbors. Last week's rainfall was a true blessing and couldn't have come at a better time. Everything seems to perk up after a refreshing rain, especially the mosquito population.

For all you radish lovers out there, keep that radish patch evenly moist because dry soil will give your radishes a tough, woody texture. And remember that the longer the radish stays in the ground, the stronger it tastes. Pluck them out often and before they get too big. I'm not a radish connoisseur, but even I can delight in a garden radish sandwich— thin slices of radish on a slice of fresh homemade bread with a thin slab of butter! Yum!

One of the finest brews available to us gardeners is manure tea. It's easy to make. Just take a large garbage can (30 gal. or so), pitch in 4 to 5 shovels of old manure and fill it with water. Swirl it around a few times and then let it steep for a couple of weeks. Plants love this nitrogen-rich drink, but mix it half and half with water or you could burn your plants. Since I don't have a horse or cow in the pasture, I have to rely on store-bought manure that comes in plastic bags. It will still make a reasonably good "cup" of tea, but somehow the aroma won't be quite the same!

46

FLOWERS FEED HUMMERS

Every summer we look forward to the visits from one of our favorite feathered friends. This teensy creature flits around our deck like lightning, sampling from the pots of nearby flowers. Maybe we enjoy these birds so much because they remind us of ourselves. How often do I seem to zip around the kitchen at 100 miles an hour while in reality I'm only hovering by the sink? How many times have I forgotten the words to an old-time tune and just had to hum along? How many nibbles do I sneak during the day in order to keep up my energy and satisfy my sweet tooth? Of course I'm referring to the acrobatic, feisty hummingbird, the only bird that can fly backwards and upside down.

This year, instead of just hanging out a plastic feeder filled with sugar water, let's plant flowers for our ruby-throated friends. But we'll have to be patient. Sometimes it takes several years to attract these gorgeous creatures. Hummingbirds are selective when it comes to their dining pleasures. We need to provide a good menu for them. And their appetites are enormous! They have to eat at least 5 times an hour to maintain their high metabolism. This calls for a lot of flowers!

Hummers prefer sweet, tubular, red flowers. If we keep these three points in mind when planting our flowers this year, we may find these iridescent beauties feeding around our gardens. One feeding empties a flower blossom for an entire day, so to keep them satisfied and happy we'll need to plant more than one window box. Other bright colors will attract hummers, but it's a good idea to start out with red, orange and rose flowers so hummers find us easily. Once we're on their route they'll continue to stop by since they have fantastic memories for good-tasting nectar.

When planning our hummingbird gardens we need to remember that hummingbirds arrive early in the season and stay late (like those relatives that came for fishing opener and stayed for the Fourth of July parade!). This means we need to have flowers blooming for the entire growing season, something that takes a good gardening plan.

Hummers absolutely love petunias, four o'clocks, impatiens, nasturtiums, snapdragons, flowering tobacco, zinnias and salvia. These annuals are easy to grow in both containers and garden plots. Be sure to plant the red and orange varieties. If you have room for only a couple of these, choose impatiens and salvia, the first for shade, the second for sun. The hummingbird's needlelike bill and long tongue are designed for the long reach into these flower cylinders. Other birds and insects can't compete when it comes to this long stretch for nectar. The biennial, foxglove, is an early summer favorite. The list of perennials is long, and if we plan carefully, will give good eating over a long period of time. Columbine and bleeding hearts are early bloomers while bee balm, coral bells, butterfly weed, phlox, dahlias and glads keep on blooming until frost. Fuchsias that make such spectacular hanging baskets by our front porch are a hummer's delight.

Several vining flowers are perfect for hummers. Dropmore honeysuckle, morning glory, scarlet runner beans and trumpet creepers come to mind. Our garden plants should also include some flowering shrubs. Honeysuckles and cardinal shrubs are two that have red and/or pink blossoms and tube-like flowers.

Avoid the newer double-flowered varieties of flowers such as the double impatiens. The nectar source in these fuller blooms is difficult for the birds to locate. This yummy flower nectar is mainly simple sugar, equivalent to a solution of 4 parts water to 1 part sugar. Even though it draws many insects, the nectar in tubular flowers is often available only to hummingbirds with their long bill. If an occasional spider or other small insect gets in the hummer's way, it makes a quick meal of it and then has a sweet drink to top off the protein course.

Hang your hummingbird feeder filled with sugar water close to your potted plants and hanging baskets. Change the water often, even if they don't drink it down, and scrub out the feeder with soap and water. Never use honey as a sugar substitute because it can make the birds ill. It takes fields of flowers to keep one hummer fed well every day, so don't despair if you have to share these feathery friends with your neighbors.

FLAVOR FOOD WITH FLOWERS

Let's do more with our flowers than just look at them. Let's eat them! Flowers not only decorate the dishes we prepare, but they also can lend a distinctive flavor. Which ones should we use and which are best left blooming in our gardens?

Many of us use nasturtium blossoms in salads. With their bright colors and sharp flavor, they are a great addition to a bowl of summer greens. I add the flowers AFTER tossing the greens with a light dressing. Float nasturtium blossoms face up on the surface of a chilled, refreshing soup like gazpacho or vichyssoise. Make a jar of flavored vinegar by loosely packing a quart jar with nasturtium blossoms, filling the jar with cider vinegar, and placing the covered jar on a shelf for a month. Use this vinegar in salad dressings.

For a special treat the next time you serve brunch to your next-door neighbors, fill individual gladioli or day lilies with servings of seafood salad or marshmallow/cream cheese dip for fruits. Hollyhocks can also be used. Won't they look spectacular on the serving plate, colorful and frilly?

I read recently that marigolds can be used in place of saffron as a flavoring for rice dishes. Although I haven't tried this, I plan to do so considering the high cost of saffron. A few threads of this herb which is harvested from the saffron crocus cost several dollars. The reason it's so pricey is that it takes 35,000 flowers to produce just 1 pound of saffron. Here are the instructions for making marigold saffron according to the May 1993 issue of *Country Journal*. Rinse and drain the entire blossom. Chop off the white bottom heel. Separate the flower into petals and spread them on a tray. Cover the petals with a paper towel and put the tray in a warm, dry place until they are dry. Crush the petals and store them in a tightly covered container. A teaspoon of dried petals added to the cooking water when preparing rice will add a gold color and pungent taste. As soon as my marigolds start to bloom, I'll have to try this.

Let's not overlook the fluffy, purple chive flowers. Toss them in salads, or garnish dishes with them. They make especially good herb vinegar, too. Use them freshly cut rather than dried when they tend to lose their color and appeal.

Johnny-jump-ups and their relatives, the violets, are especially attractive on our dinner plates as well as in our yards and gardens. Their bright faces liven up just about any dull fare. I recall the lively discussion these jump-ups prompted at a birthday gathering with friends a couple years ago. The hostess, who always has a lovely garden, had sprinkled some Johnny faces on top of the green salad she had made from garden greens. It was the hit of the party! Now we guests are always on the alert for Sally's creative additions whenever we dine at her home.

For a simple yet colorful surprise, add a Johnny-jump-up to each cell of the ice cube tray. Add water, freeze, and then float the cubes in a tall, cool drink. These flowered cubes show up the best if we use clear serving glasses.

It seems almost cruel and insensitive to eat roses. Yet those of us with shrub roses can easily find some extra blossoms that we can use in the kitchen. Rose petals mixed in with softened butter/margarine make a spread that's tasty on muffins and breads. Add petals to pancake and muffin batters, or toss petals with fresh fruit and sprinkle with freshly squeezed lime or orange juice or a few squirts of ginger ale. If you have the patience of a saint, you might want to make candied rose petals or flowers. To make the coating, add 1 1/2 tsp finely granulated sugar to an egg white and beat the white until it's frothy. Dip the flowers into the mixture. Then dust them with finely granulated sugar. Place the flowers or petals on waxed paper and let them dry until they're brittle. This works the best when days are dry and airy, not humid and sticky. Store them in a tightly covered container.

Always choose flowers that are the freshest and brightest. If they're wilted in the garden, they'll be even more wilted on the salad plate! Harvest them in the morning before the hot sun has dried them out. Remove the pistils and stamens from flowers like lilies and hollyhocks. Rinse the flowers gently in cool water and store them in a covered container in the refrigerator. Never use flowers that have been sprayed with a pesticide.

Choose flowers that you know are edible. In addition to the ones I've already mentioned, SAFE flowers to eat include asters, bachelor buttons, begonias, dahlias, daisies, impatiens and petunias. According to the Minnesota Poison Control Center, these flowers are NOT SAFE to eat: foxglove, iris, azalea, daffodil, lily of the valley, delphinium, larkspur, sweet pea, four o'clock, lobelia, monkshood, and morning glory.

Strawberry picking season is that time of year when we gorge ourselves on shortcake for breakfast, lunch and dinner! Quickly rinse the fresh berries in cold water. Don't let them soak in the sink while you're removing the stems. Use a potato peeler rather than a paring knife to remove stems. The cupped point on the peeler easily pulls out the pulpy stem and the sharp edge will clip off any soft spots.

We should keep a lookout for leaf spot diseases. Remove and destroy any spotted, yellowing leaves on the lower parts of tomato plants to discourage the spread of diseases. Overhead watering causes dirt to splash up on plants so soil-born diseases get off to a good start. There's not much we can do with Mother Nature's rain showers except plant in plastic. So far my plants look healthy, but there's no telling when fungi will take off and grow.

Remember to remove old blossoms from annual and perennial flowers to prevent seed and encourage more blooms. This is especially important with geraniums, petunias and cutting flowers such as zinnias. Snip off faded peonies. Fertilize roses every month until late summer.

SEPTORIA AND SUCKERS KEEP GARDENERS BUSY IN JULY

Septoria. Sounds like a summer vacation destination, possibly with a pretty waterfall, bed and breakfast mansions offering scones and tea in the afternoons, nearby orchards where you could pick your own ripe fruit of the season. Surprise! Septoria is the name given to one of the most common fungal leaf spot diseases affecting our tomatoes. Blight is the catch-all term we use when we refer to these fungal diseases. Regardless of the name, these tomato diseases drive us gardeners crazy during the wet days of July when temps range between 60 and 80 degrees.

The first symptoms we see are brown spots on the lower leaves of our tomato plants. Quickly the leaves will yellow. Some will drop off. Sometimes the entire plant will lose all of its leaves and the tomatoes are left hanging on all alone with no protection from the sun or leaves to make food. Plants suffering from septoria leaf blight usually produce some fruit, but production is often way down and fruit ripens all at once.

Why do we get blight on our tomatoes year after year? Because it's in the soil that our plants call "home." Blight also winters over on plant refuse that we leave in our gardens. It spreads the next season by water splashing up from this contaminated soil during rains/watering and by us gardeners working among wet plants. Blight can stay alive in the soil for years.

Since the disease starts on the lower leaves, we can often save the rest of the plant by applying a fungicide on the plants when we first see signs of the disease. I often start a spraying program even before I see evidence of the disease. If the weather this time of year is especially wet and nothing, including my laundry on the line, ever dries off, then I suspect my tomato plants will soon be in trouble. Fungicides won't destroy the organisms already on the infected leaves, but will discourage it from spreading up to healthy leaves. Tomato plants without leaves won't have any way of producing food for the plant, so it's important that we save the upper leaves if we want any tomatoes. If you decide to spray with a fungicide, be sure to read the label first to find out if the spray is intended for use on tomatoes. Then follow directions exactly. One spraying won't be enough, so be prepared for long-term duty.

There are a couple things we gardeners can do to deter the spreading of this disease once our plants are in the ground. First, we need to remove all diseased tomato leaves and plants from our gardens as soon as possible. If our plants are already infected and dropping leaves, this is a daily chore. If we have overhead watering sprinklers, we need to water in the early mornings so plants have a chance to dry off before evening. Fungi love moist areas, so by keeping plants dried off we'll help slow down the disease. This alone won't stop the disease once it has started, though. Rotation of tomatoes from one spot to another in our gardens is a good idea, but many of us small-time gardeners just don't have the space for this. If you have the room, it's always a good practice to rotate vegetable crops every year.

Mention the word "sucker" in this part of the country and most folks think you're talking about a bottom feeding fish that we throw back if it lands on our fishing line. In garden lingo, a sucker is part of a plant that produces little but sucks off lots of nutrients. In either language, it's usually an undesirable something-or-other that needs to be discarded, whether from our fishing line or our tomato plants.

Tomato plants produce lots of suckers. Left unpruned, these suckers grow and can become large stems with suckers of their own. Whether or not you want to prune them off is your decision, but there are some points to consider while deciding what to do.

Suckers grow out from the stem right above the leaf branch in the Y formed by the stem and branch. Why remove them? Suckers add a lot of extra foliage to tomato plants. If this foliage is removed, ventilation around the plant is improved, which helps prevent disease. The plant is opened up to more sunlight, which warms the plant and helps in ripening the tomatoes. Suckers often develop their own blossoms and fruits. More plant energy is then directed to the suckers and less to the main stems and branches which are fruited as well. This usually means that you may have more tomatoes but they will be smaller in size.

Suckers aren't all bad. They provide more foliage to help the plant make food. They also shade tomatoes from the sun. This is especially important in hot parts of the country where the bright sun actually burns tomatoes.

New suckers form quickly in the heat and humidity. We need to be on the lookout for them every few days during this time of fast growth. All we need to do is pinch them off using our thumb and forefinger.

It's time for me to cover my cabbage heads to keep the cabbage worm off them. Guess what I'm going to use. Old panty hose! Better to have them on cabbages than my legs, especially now that summer has arrived with its warmth and stickiness! The hose will stretch as the cabbage heads enlarge. Some gardeners place fine netting over their cole crops to prevent the cabbage butterflies from laying their eggs on the plants. If you have many plants, it's best to use a row cover that is sold by the yard and can be stretched out the entire length of your crop. There are covers commercially available for this purpose. But for the four cabbages I squeezed into my garden, panty hose will be just fine! Keep an eye open for the creamy white cabbage butterfly. Once we see them dancing above our gardens, it's time for action.

My favorite flower thus far this season? Datura, commonly called Angel's Trumpet, is a hands-down winner! Its pure white blooms are breathtakingly beautiful. They are about 5 inches across and exude a sweet perfume that's especially intense during sunset hours. The plant stands tall at around 3 feet in a container on our deck. It needs full sun and is a fast grower, and if planted directly in a garden it will achieve even greater heights. The attractive leaves have a bluish cast. For drama and fragrance, consider sowing your own seeds next spring.

SLUGGING IT OUT

When cool, moist weather hangs around, we can expect lengthy visits from some uninvited guests—and I don't mean our long lost cousins! I'm talking about slugs, those slimy, slick members of the mollusk family that live on the land, not in the water.

Slugs are snails without shells. Their slippery bodies can be anywhere from 1 to 8 inches long although in our part of the country they're usually between 1 and 2 inches. Aren't we lucky? As for color, they're usually a grayish tan, sometimes with black spots. Again, this can vary. But take my word for it, they're definitely unattractive, no matter what color! Actually, unless we're prowling about late at night, we won't bump into them, as they do their dirty deeds like most other thieves and outlaws under the cloak of darkness. Once the sun starts to shine, they decide to take their day-long snooze, hiding beneath a nearby board or debris.

Slugs love moist, well-mulched gardens. Common sense tells us they're more likely to do damage in our shady gardens where they get shelter from the sun. Nothing suits their fancy more than juicy hosta leaves, although they aren't particularly fussy and will make dinner out of almost anything. Often they start nibbling on the lower, slightly rotting leaves and then venture upward. While they have a definite fondness for hollyhocks, delphiniums, snapdragons, begonias, pansies and petunias, they'll also devour cabbage, daylilies and marigolds. Trying to plant what they don't like is out of the question! During a dry season, we won't be bothered by them, but with rainy weather, watch out!

Slugs aren't neat eaters. They leave large, ragged holes in leaves and sometimes even eat the entire leaf. Be on the lookout for their trail. Instead of footprints, they leave a line of slime on the soil around plants and on leaves.

What can we do about a slug invasion? The best prevention starts in the fall when the gardening season is over. That's the time to get rid of all garden debris, nearby weeds and junk that often accumulates around our gardens. The fewer places available for over-wintering protection, the fewer slugs will survive. I wish I could say that a spray is available that will wipe them off the face of the earth, but there isn't one! Their ability to play hide-and-seek with us makes them about impossible to eliminate. But don't despair! There are ways we can control them, although they aren't for the weak-kneed or faint-of-heart.

BARRIERS are anything that will protect our plants from being reached by slugs. Diatomaceous Earth (D.E. for short) is a powder made from the fossilized skeletons of microscopic sea creatures. It seems rather ho-hum to us, but to the soft-bodied slugs that hope to crawl over it, it's like hot coals. This D.E. has sharp edges that will cut the outer membranes of any soft-skinned critters. To apply, dust D.E. around the base of plants and continue upward from the ground, covering stems and leaves. The nuisance with this powder is that it must be reapplied after every rainfall. Crushed eggshells make a formidable barrier. Sprinkle them as deeply as possible around your favorite plants. Other suggested barriers are chicken grit, wood ashes (a handful or two around a large plant is all that's advised) and sharp sand.

BAITS and TRAPS are available commercially but we can also make our own. The most common bait and one of the most effective is the beer trap. Locate a straight-sided container, either plastic or tin, with a plastic lid. Cut a 2-inch hole out of the plastic lid. Pour an inch or two of beer into the container, snap on the lid and bury it in the soil near the affected plants, keeping it flush with the surface so the slugs can easily climb in. They'll drown in the beer. Another trap using beer or any other slug bait can be easily made from a large plastic pop bottle. Cut the top 1/3 off the bottle. Invert this section back into the rest of the bottle, attaching it with staples. Pour the bait into the bottle and lay the bottle horizontally on top of the soil, pushing it down in an inch or two so it doesn't blow away. Slugs will crawl into the bottle but won't be able to crawl back out. Keep in mind that these traps need to be monitored daily. Empty dead slugs and add some fresh beer. Gardeners have also had good luck using yeast as bait. Add water to ordinary kitchen-type yeast and pour it into the trap. Any old board, shingle, piece of carpet or hollowed-out grapefruit can serve as a trap, a cool, shady environment as cover for the slugs taking a snooze. Just lay them around the area in your garden where you suspect slug action. Check under the traps several times a day for slugs. Pick them up (I always use a tweezer!) and drop them into a container of soap and water.

Commercial baits are available at garden centers. I've heard good results from those that are sprinkled on the ground around plants that slugs love. Follow directions carefully, and if you have dogs or other pets, be sure the baits won't harm them.

HANDPICKING can make a sizeable dent in the slug population if you don't mind grabbing their slimy bodies! It's much more fun picking strawberries, trust me! Here's where a pair of rubber gloves comes in handy. I absolutely refuse to touch these critters, so I use an old pair of long-handled tweezers. Chopsticks will work, too. If you're lucky to have kids nearby, a little financial incentive might be in order, say a nickel apiece or whatever your finances can afford.

Last of all, welcome friends into your garden that dine on slugs. Toads, snakes and robins (and other garden birds) find slugs a tasty treat and are happy to bite into a nice juicy slug. This means you'll have to go easy on the use of other pesticides which may be toxic to these helpful creatures.

Thinking about toads reminds me of a scene when I was out in the front yard with my canine pals, Sophie and Gus. Sophie had come upon a large toad in the grass, sneaking cautiously up to it only to have it jump up in her face. She took a quick leap backward, then sneaked up again. The same thing happened: toad leaped, Sophie jumped, then her nose led her back to the toad. They played this funny game for several minutes until I called her into the house. Toads are a gardeners good friend. They eat hundreds of insects every night including slugs, grubs, grasshoppers and cutworms. Make them welcome and they'll set up a home for years to come. During the day they nestle down into damp mulch or beneath low-growing plants and at night they come out to dine. Toads may be warty looking creatures, but don't worry, the warts won't spread! The old wives' tale about touching toads causing warts on humans is totally untrue.

WE ALL NEED SUPPORT NOW AND THEN

Feeling a bit droopy lately? You're not alone. Many of our perennial flowers suffer the same predicament, especially those with large, heavy blossoms, or those that are tall and thin. What we do for our own case of the droops varies. Maybe we get a hair perm, or go shopping for a new outfit, or go to lunch with a friend. What we do for our plants is to give them some means of support so they perk up and don't fall over.

Unfortunately, we often forget about lending this support until it's already too late. Peonies are a good example. As fresh sprigs shooting from the ground in the early spring, they seem sturdy enough, and it isn't until later, when they're bending to the ground with huge flowers that we realize they really aren't so sturdy after all. Delphiniums are another case. How many times have you ventured outside after a strong wind and rain, only to find them bent in half? Enough of this! Let's see how we can help.

Gardens that are protected often don't have this droopy problem. Any means of shelter from Mother Nature's elements will help maintain plants in an upright position. Fences, walls, even hedges or buildings will soften the wind and give protection to plants. Just be sure these barriers don't shut out the sunlight. Plants that have plenty of room to grow strong stems are less likely to tip over than those in crowded situations where they become spindly and weak. Plants that need plenty of sunlight will be weakened if set in the shade. So the first thing for us to consider is whether or not we are fulfilling the plant's basic needs.

Not all plants need staking. Marigolds, for example, often have large blooms, but seldom do they need our help because they grow on strong, sturdy stems with lots of foliage for added protection. Certain plants are almost destined for tipping over. In addition to peonies and delphiniums, certain tall lilies, dahlias, hollyhocks, gladiolus and plants with fragile stems such as some daisies or asters may also need a lift. The short Asiatic lilies blooming in front of my new perennial border won't need any staking, but the taller Oriental lilies, already almost 3 feet tall could be in trouble if we have a strong wind.

What methods are best for supporting plants? My advice is to check what you have on hand first. There's no sense buying things if we already have something tucked away in the garage or basement that could be used. An important consideration in my book is to choose supports that are as inconspicuous as possible. Anything loud and obnoxious will draw attention away from the flowering plant and defeats the purpose of having the plant in the first place. Garden and hardware stores carry certain types of supports for specific plants. Last year I bought a hoop made of galvanized metal that encircles a large peony plant. The plant easily camouflaged it by late May, so it became entirely hidden. Yet it has kept the plant neat and tidy. Wire cages that we use for tomatoes are often good for flowers. Open wire fencing will support sweet peas and other climbers, and traditional bamboo stakes are inconspicuous and make good supports since they come in various sizes and can be trimmed down. The general idea is to choose a support that will reach about as tall as the plant stem when it's mature. A pruned, twiggy branch from a small tree is called a "pea stick" Once inserted in the ground it hardly shows at all, and the blossom rests comfortably in the crotch of the large twig.

When we use a stake-type support we'll need to tie the plant to it or it will be useless. We have many choices for ties, but it's best to select one that won't show or damage the plant. Personally, I think this is a perfect job for old panty hose. Since I hate wearing them in the first place, this seems a perfect way to make sure they're being put to good use! Thin strips of this elastic hose are soft, and yet hold plants carefully to the stakes. Other suggestions are twines, yarn and raffia.

Because my memory plays tricks on me and plants often grow faster than I expect them to, I often stake plants as soon as I put them in the ground or when they're showing good growth in the early spring. Insert the stakes/supports about 6 inches away from the base of the plant to avoid damaging too many roots. As the plant grows, continue to tie the stem to the stake. As in the case of the peony hoops, nothing needs to be done after they're in place except to occasionally pull a heavy branch through the hoop where it belongs. In no time the foliage of the plants covers the supports and keeps them hidden from view. Staking individual stems of large clumps of delphinium, for instance, is a huge chore. An option may be to encircle several stalks with netting or fencing bent in half earlier in the growing season, and unfolding the support as the plants grow. Fencing behind plants can also offer an easy way to keep them in place. This spring I planted a clematis along a split rail fence. It has climbed the piece of wire fencing I attached to the bottom of the fence and is now sprawling along the rails. It was easy, and the plant is adjusting well to the idea.

Where did all the purple go? Have you ever wondered why the luscious purple-colored asparagus comes out of the steamer a plain green? I was so disappointed the first year I grew purple-streaked green bush beans. On the vine they were so beautiful, but by the time they emerged from blanching, they had lost the purple streaks and looked just like every other green bean I'd ever planted. Fact is, the purple pigment can't take the heat. When heat hits the cells containing the purple pigment, the membranes break down and the pigment mixes with other plant juices—and no more purple! Purple peppers and purple tomatillos will undergo the same loss when cooked. Soaking the vegetables in lemon juice or vinegar overnight prior to cooking will increase the acid level and this will help sustain the purple color. But when it comes right down to it, we'd better appreciate the purple color while the vegetables are still in our gardens. The other solution is simple— eat the vegetables raw.

The guilt I experience while drinking too much coffee has suddenly vanished, ever since I read that coffee grounds are an excellent addition to the compost pile. They are a good source of nitrogen, and their damp, crumbly texture makes them easy to compost. They are acidic, so using coffee grounds as a mulch around our acid-loving blueberries, azaleas and rhododendrons is a terrific idea. So long, guilt. Bring on the cappuccino.

IRISES FORM RAINBOWS OF COLOR

Years ago I went to school with a girl named Iris. Unless my memory fails me, she was as pretty as the flower with the same name. Well, almost as pretty. Except she didn't have the beard that fringes our most popular garden irises. Lucky for her! The iris is named after the goddess of the rainbow. Can you think of a more spectacularly beautiful sight than the rainbow encircling the earth after a rain shower? True to the goddess, irises come in all colors of the rainbow except true red. One of these years that will change as hybridizers work steadily to develop one. The iris has undergone dramatic improvement and development lately. Several types are suitable for our gardens in this area. We have thousands of lovely varieties in a complete range of colors, sizes and forms from which to choose. Now is the time to get them started.

Irises are dormant from mid-July until the first of September. We want to take advantage of this sleeping time to transplant irises so they will have time to develop new root systems and become established before winter sets in. Of course this is also the time when we gardeners are knee-deep in picking beans, making zucchini pickles, struggling to stay ahead of weeds, and freezing broccoli. What ever happened to the lazy, hazy days of summer? Many of us are lucky enough to get some divisions of irises from friends who are breaking up 4 to 5-year-old clumps that have become too crowded. A spading fork is a terrific tool to have in hand for this job. Lift the entire clump and try not to break the feeder roots. Wash off the soil and separate the rhizomes (root-like stems) into individual fans with a sharp knife. Toss the center divisions that bloomed this spring and use only the vigorous, healthy-looking fans. Cut the leaves back to about 6 inches and trim off any broken roots. Dip the rhizomes in a solution of about 3 tablespoons Lysol to a gallon of water, or in a good fungicide such as Captan. Let the entire plant dry. Then it's ready for planting.

Most irises like lots of sunlight and well-drained soil. There are some, like the Siberian Iris, that prefer moist soil. Know which you are planting before you choose a site. If your soil drains poorly, you would be better off making a raised bed for your irises. A low spot where rain collects after a shower could be fatal for most irises. Prepare the soil as you would for any new planting. Remove weeds, dig deeply, and work in lots of organic matter. Fresh manure could cause root rot, so don't use it. Manure needs to be old and decomposed well before we use it around our plants. You might want to add a complete fertilizer that's high in phosphorus and potassium (the 2nd and 3rd numbers on the fertilizer bag). Bonemeal, which we can buy in garden centers is a terrific additive to soil when we are planting any bulbs or rhizomes.

Plant irises with the rhizome just below the soil surface. In sandy soil the rhizome may be a little deeper, but not over 1 inch. Again, this might vary with the species, so follow any special directions that come with your plant. Dig a large hole and leave a ridge of soil down the center. Put the rhizome on top of this ridge, with the roots fanning out on both sides. Check the depth to be sure the rhizome won't be too deep. Firm the soil over the roots and rhizome and add water to settle the soil. Don't water much again until you see some new top growth which tells us that the roots have become established. Give irises plenty of space because they spread quickly. Leave at least 8 inches between fans. The newer hybrids don't increase as quickly so they can be planted a couple inches closer together.

Everything around here can use some winter protection and irises are no exception. We can't always depend on snow cover to help us out. After the first frost this fall, cut the leaves back to about 6 inches. This will get rid of some diseases that may be on the leaves. Spray with a good fungicide and insecticide if you want to forestall any problems that may develop. Apply the mulch some time in November, once we've had several hard frosts. Use at least 6 to 8 inches of clean straw, or some other non-packing material.

Siberian irises are another story. They have fibrous roots, grass-like leaves, and prefer a moist site. They will do well in a mixed flower garden provided they receive enough moisture in the spring. Spring is the best time to divide and plant this kind of iris. Like the bearded iris, the Siberian iris grows in clumps and needs to be divided every 4 to 5 years for best growth. Its flowers are usually white, blue or yellow.

Check your roses for black spot. This is one of the most common diseases of roses and usually comes about when we have wet weather, extra humidity, and heavy dew. Look for black spots about 1/16 to 1/2 inches in diameter. Infected leaves turn yellow and drop off. This could rob the rose of the leaves needed to give energy for good growth. There are some things we gardeners can do to help prevent this disease. We should avoid any conditions that allow rose foliage to remain wet for long periods of time—crowding of plants, too much shade, overhead watering, and watering at night. If black spot is a problem, we need to remove and destroy the infected leaves. We might want to use a registered fungicide for best control at this point. There are many available on the market.

RIPE, SWEET, AND READY TO EAT!

Fresh corn on the cob is always best. If we're growing it, we know we're cooking and eating as fresh as it gets! But if we are buying it, how can we tell a fresh ear from one that's not so fresh?

Look at the husks. They should be green and moist. If they're drying out, chances are the kernels inside are drying out as well and won't be juicy and tender. Feel of the ear for kernels. The ear should be well filled clear up to the tip. Try not to peel back the husks too far as they keep the ear plump and fresh. With a bit of practice, we'll know "just by feeling" which ears are full and which are not. If you see some signs of corn earworms at the tips, don't assume the ear is bad. Just cut off these tips before preparing the ears for supper.

There are some terrific recipes for fresh corn, but truth is, ON THE COB is everyone's favorite way to eat sweet corn until the season is well underway and we want to try something a bit different. Here up north the corn season is so short that we rarely tire of gnawing off those succulent, sweet kernels from the cob.

Fresh corn popped into a kettle of boiling water needs only 3 to 4 minutes until it's hot and tender enough to be lifted out onto our plates. Adding salt to the cooking water will toughen the corn so keep the shaker on the table and away from the cookstove.

Some cooks rely on their microwaves for cooking corn, loosely wrapping each ear in plastic wrap or leaving the ear in its husk for the duration. Cooking time will vary, depending on the power of the microwave and the number of ears being cooked at one time.

Grilled corn is really tasty. Carefully pull back the husks to remove the silks. Then soak the entire ear, husks and all, in cool water for 1/2 hour. Pull the husks back up over the ear to cover it, twist the top closed as tightly as you can, and place it on the grill. If you like, peel back the husks once more and brown the ears slightly on the grill right before serving.

Melons are another story. Have you ever watched shoppers in the grocery store looking for a ripe melon? It's almost a comic routine! They each have their own unique way of testing a melon for ripeness. Some shake the melons, others sniff them, while the next shopper knocks gently on them with a knuckle, keeping an ear next to the melon in hopes of hearing some magical sound. Then again, there's the occasional shopper that foregoes all of the above and just grabs the first one on the pile.

Selecting ripe muskmelons is easier to me than finding the best watermelon. We need only our eyes and noses. A ripe one has a full, fruity fragrance which any unplugged nose can detect. It helps to have the fruit at room temperature and not refrigerated. As to color, the tan netting on many muskmelons becomes more pronounced and the background color changes from a green to a yellowish color.

The problem when selecting a ripe watermelon is that the plant provides most of the clues to ripeness, but in the grocery store, we're out of luck! If you have them in your garden, check the curly tendril right by the spot where the melon attaches to the stem. It should be dead or brown, not green. As to color, a ripe melon becomes less shiny bright green as it matures. Instead of being glossy, it turns a dull green. This takes a bit of practice to determine. Some folks swear by the thumping routine, as a ripe melon gives out a low-pitched sound when thumped. I'm not good at this, I'll admit, but some folks swear by it. As for the undersides of the melon, the color will vary. A seedless variety will be tinged yellow in this area when it's ripe. The seeded varieties will be creamy white. Again, we need to know what kind of watermelon we're buying so we will know this difference. One thing I know for certain. I prefer my muskmelons at room temperature for the best taste. If they're cool, they're refreshing but their flavor doesn't come out as well. The same for watermelons, in my opinion. But on a hot summer's day, cold fruit is what we reach for, and seems to appease our thirsts. So go for it!

Here's a quick note on pesticide use. If you're doing any dusting or spraying this season of your fruits, vegetables and flowers, be sure to at least wear protective gloves before handling these materials. It's always a good idea to pull on a coverall of some kind, too, but many times we think we're in too much of a hurry for all this rigamarole. If we can keep our hands from coming in contact with these pesticides, we're taking a big step toward keeping pesticides off our bodies. Follow directions carefully when using any of these chemicals, and be sure to reach for those gloves.

Have you heard of a perennial flower called Lady's Mantle? I was fortunate to find a good buy on one of these plants this spring, and added it to my perennial collection. The feature that makes lady's mantle (*Alchemilla mollis*) so valuable to us gardeners is that it's shade tolerant. In fact, I tucked it in a moist area beneath a tree along the west side of our yard and it's doing well. Lady's mantle is not as showy a plant as is the Oriental lily in full bloom that perfumes the entire front yard. It's beauty lies in its outstanding foliage and lovely, delicate yellow-green flowers that rise above the foliage on tall stems, much like coral bells. These airy clouds of chartreuse flowers make excellent fillers in flower arrangements and have a long vase life. Lady's mantle forms a mound of foliage, spreading about 18 inches. The large leaves are rounded with scalloped lobes. Because the foliage is covered with many fine hairs, it has almost a velvety look. On a dewy morning droplets hang onto the leaves, glistening in the early sunlight. It's a lovely sight! We can use lady's mantle in several ways—as a contrast in perennial beds with such upright plants as Siberian iris, or veronica, or as a ground cover. It also makes a nice edging plant along pathways. It prefers cool, moist weather so keep it watered frequently during dry spells. In our cooler climate, it even tolerates full sun but needs plenty of mulch to keep the soil from drying out.

PRESERVE THE FRESHNESS

Blanch and I spent a busy weekend together. While she sputtered and popped her lid over preparing broccoli for the freezer, I sat in a rocking chair watching old westerns and breaking string beans. It was one of those weekends when all else came to a screeching halt. TV dinners for supper; store-bought cookies to dunk in coffee; shorter-than-usual morning dog walks. Everyone sacrifices when it's canning and freezing time around here.

We can freeze most vegetables and know they'll be safe to eat. But first we need to BLANCH them. This process of dunking clean, raw vegetables in a pot of boiling water for a specified time is called blanching. Check a good cookbook for this blanching time. It will vary with the vegetables you are freezing, and the size and shape they're in (whole versus small pieces). It's important that you blanch in a large kettle with enough hot water so that the water doesn't cool off when the vegetables are added. We want to keep those bubbles jumping, just as though we were cooking spaghetti. When the time is up, plunge those vegetables in cold—and I mean ICY cold—water. This will stop the cooking process immediately and keep those vegetables at top quality in our freezers. Drain the veggies well. I blot them dry with paper towels to cut down on the ice crystals that form when the veggies are placed in the freezer. I've had good luck spreading beans and broccoli on cookie sheets and placing them in the freezer. When they are frozen I break them apart and put them in large plastic bags. Then I take out only the amount we'll use for a meal and reseal the bag. Get as much air out of the storage containers as you possibly can. Air left in with the produce will only take away from its freshness and flavor. It's easy to press air out of plastic bags, but the only way to eliminate air from rigid containers is to fill them quite full.

Soak your broccoli in cold salt water for at least half an hour before blanching it. This will chase out any cabbage worms that may be nestled in the florets. Pick broccoli while the florets are still tightly closed. Don't wait until yellow buds and flowers appear. Instead of discarding the heavy stem of the broccoli, peel off the outer skin and cut the crisp, juicy inner stalk into strips to add to salad. It's delicious! Just ask our three dogs who beg by the kitchen sink! They know a tasty morsel when they taste one! We never have any of these strips left to add to salads.

The only way zucchini freezes well is if you grate it first and press out a lot of the moisture. If you find an overgrown club full of seeds hiding under a leaf one morning when you check out your garden, grate it up. Take out the seeds first. Soak up the moisture with paper towels, and put the zucchini into small containers. Reach for them the next time you bake muffins, breads or cakes.

Annual flowers such as alyssum, violas and petunias tend to get a bit scraggly this time of year. If we trim them back a little they will bloom again in a couple of weeks and keep blooming longer into the late summer. It's not easy to cut off petunias that are blooming their hearts out, but they'll be perky for several days in a vase of lukewarm water on our kitchen counters. Trim snapdragons way back after they have bloomed and they will send out new buds and flower well until a killing frost.

Tomatoes are really the best eaten right off the vine. Sliced tomatoes drizzled with a bit of olive oil and a dash of salt and pepper can't be topped! Or how about making a quick bruschetta for lunch this weekend? Toast a slice of sturdy, coarse bread (forget about the gooey, fine white stuff!). Rub it with a half clove of garlic. Then press half of a small, fresh tomato into the toasted bread until it has almost turned to sauce. Add a few drops of olive oil and top it with salt and pepper and grated mozzarella or your favorite cheese. That's it, easy and delicious!

When the hot, dog days of summer set in it's a good idea to set our lawn mower blades slightly higher. If the mower cuts too closely, our lawn will have a tendency to brown out faster in the heat. The Minnesota Extension Service advises us to quit bagging grass clippings and to leave these clippings on our yards to decompose instead. They will not add to thatch problems because thatch consists of roots and stems that decompose very slowly. Grass clippings break down quickly and add nutrients to the soil. The key to success is to mow often so we never have to remove more than 1/3 of the grass height at any given time. This sounds downright unrealistic at times when we are busy with summer chores. But at least we know how it should be done and we can work at it. If you have a bagging mower and want to use it without the bag, fit it with a safety device to keep it from picking up stones and shooting them out where they can injure someone.

BACKYARD BANDITS

Who's coming to dinner? Is it Mr. Rabbit? Or perhaps the petunia nibbler is Chatty Chipmunk. It's easy to blame Rambunctious Raccoon who raids bird feeders and garbage cans. After all, he doesn't wear that mask for nothing! Then again, let's blame the acrobatic Mr. Deer who, with superman-like prowess, can leap tall fences in a single bound. Whoever they are helping themselves to our gardens, they aren't welcome! We'd hang out a sign saying "Restaurant Closed!" if only they could read. What's a gardener to do? Will there be any harvest left for us planters?

City and country dwellers alike report the same mystery: who is responsible for our disappearing flowers and veggies during the middle of the night? If it's any consolation, we're not in this alone. The increasing populations of deer throughout the country lead to lots of gardener frustration. And the more we choose to build our dream houses in remote areas where wildlife abounds—and let's face it, the abundance of animals and nature has a lot to do with the desirability of housing sites—the more we gardeners have to deal with feeding them, whether by invitation or not.

We can usually determine the culprit by assessing the damage. Nipped off lily buds are likely eaten by deer who are tall enough to reach them. Pansy flowers, which, incidentally, taste good in our supper salads, are equally tempting to rabbits and chipmunks. Melons with gnawed holes and scooped out fruit have been dinner to racoons who, with their dextrous paws, stop at nothing to get at their favorite delicacy. Identifying the culprit is step #1. Then maybe, and it's a big MAYBE, we can get to step #2, stopping the damage.

Gardeners devise oodles of ingenious ways to keep ahead of rabbits, chipmunks, raccoons and deer. Unfortunately, most of them don't work for long. Hair clippings from ourselves and our dogs, strong smelling soaps, blood meal, commercial repellents, even high tech devices that supposedly emit sound waves that are unbearable to animals—all have us hopeful but eventually disappointed. They may help us win an occasional battle, but the war continues. When all is said and done, there are maybe three significant measures we can take that are most effective.

Fences and other barriers—Electric fences will usually keep deer and bear out IF they're at the right height to zap their tender noses and ears. The rest of their hide is so tough that they'll ignore most electric zings. A wide area of woven wire fencing (5 feet minimum) laid FLAT around the perimeter of a garden is said to keep deer out because they don't like to step through it and can't jump across it easily. A two-strand electric fence with one strand lower to the ground will discourage raccoons and porcupines. Rabbits are stopped by common chicken wire mesh fencing, but remember to dig it into the ground a few inches because rabbits will dig under it. Another barrier is netting to keep our feathered friends off our ripening fruit. The only other creatures that appreciate berries and apples more than we are the birds! While it isn't easy to cover a fruit tree with netting (definitely a two-person task), it's more effective than plastic snakes or aluminum pie plates dangling in the breeze. Monofilament line (thick fishing line) strung close to the ground around plants is also reported to stop deer since their feet tangle in it and it confuses them because they can't see it. It's worth a try, especially if you don't have time to go fishing.

Dogs—Most gardeners who have canine friends also have critter-controllers. Our dogs are always within their fenced yard except for occasional forays into the front yard/garden for a quick romp. Their scent along the yard perimeter seems to be enough to at least make the deer stop and think first about venturing in. As a caution, don't let your dogs roam freely without supervision to patrol and chase whatever shows up. In the first place, they run the risk of being hurt themselves—by road traffic and porcupines, which can wreck a dog's life forever. Secondly, dogs quickly discover the great sport of chasing deer, which is illegal in the state. This can result in a mess of trouble with the law and neighbors. On the other hand, our terriers, diggers through and through, keep our fenced yard free of chipmunks and rabbits. As a gardener, I benefit from their help, and yard hunting keeps them entertained for hours.

Traps—Chipmunks are cute little buggers but can do a swift number on flower buds. If you've noticed disbudding of garden flowers, suspect chipmunks. Rather than killing them off or leaving them for Gus the schnauzer to terrorize, we live-trapped two dozen last year, letting them free on nearby state-owned land, and the population has been under control ever since. Traps sometimes work for woodchucks, wily characters that laugh out loud at fences which, of course, they quickly tunnel underneath. Desperate gardeners also resort to bombs made especially for burrowing creatures. Check local ordinances first before desperation drives you to use bad judgement!

Milorganite—a commercially produced organic fertilizer made from septic sludge, repels many animals when it's sprinkled on the ground around plants. Unfortunately, it loses its effectiveness when plants get taller and animals don't have to stoop low to nibble on them. Milorganite, available in granular form, is sold in garden centers. Remember that this product takes the fun out of stopping to smell the flowers for us humans as well since the odor is awful! Every year there are new sprays and repellents on the market. One that our local Soil and Water Conservation Department deems effective is called Plantskyyd. For one thing, it won't harm animals or plants because the active ingredient is pig blood. Also, it won't wash off in the rain. New applications need to be made on new growth; otherwise, two to three sprays a year are usually enough to ward off deer.

Maybe the best thing for us to do is to learn to live with these critters. This involves sharing harvest and not getting too upset when nature's wildlife decides to savor our garden delicacies. I know this is easier said than done, especially when they devour our expensive hosta or our entire field of sweet corn in one evening. Maybe a longer fall hunting season is in order!

TOOT YOUR HORN FOR FRESH GARDEN CORN!

I'm not a corn grower. A corn eater? You bet! But a grower? No. In a small garden like mine, it just doesn't work. And besides, we're only a short distance from our local Farmers' Markets which have several varieties of the best corn for miles—and lots of it! But I know, just by driving around the countryside, that many gardeners have a few rows on one side of their plots designated for sweet corn. My hat's off to you! Getting corn to the table isn't easy. Harvesting those sweet, succulent ears before the raccoons, deer and squirrels do is nothing short of a miracle.

Corn isn't really hard to grow. Once it gets plenty of sun and heat, it shoots for the sky. We've all heard tales about farmers who claim to be able to hear corn growing during the warm, sultry days. Any plant that grows so tall so quickly needs plenty of fertilizer and requires good, nourishing soil. Many corn gardeners apply a side dressing of high nitrogen fertilizer alongside the corn rows mid-season.

A member of the grass family, corn can't tolerate frost and shouldn't be planted until the ground warms up in late spring. A good seed soaking for 24 hours before planting speeds up germination. Plants need to be at least a foot apart, but since germination is around 75%, it's a good idea to seed closer and thin later. Rather than a few long rows, plant corn in several short rows or blocks. Corn is pollinated not by insects but by the wind, and common sense tells us that the closer together the rows, the better the pollination and production.

Corn has a big thirst as well as a big appetite. A minimum of an inch of water a week is a must, especially once the corn is tasseling which signals ears being filled with kernels.

The confusing part for beginning corn growers is which type to grow. What's the difference between sugary, sugar enhanced and the new supersweets? It can be a puzzle indeed. Here are the basics. SU is the code for "SUGARY". These are the old types of sweet corn whose sugar converts quickly to starch, hence the need to pick and freeze (or eat!) in a hurry. These varieties are hardy and disease resistant, and include Honey and Cream (bicolor) and Silver Queen (white).

SE cultivars are sweeter than the sugary ones. The SE stands for "SUGAR ENHANCED". They don't go starchy as fast as the old varieties and are sweeter. Some popular ones include Kandy King (yellow), Lancelot (bicolor) and Platinum Lady (white).

SH2 are the new "SUPERSWEET" varieties, and an appropriate name it is! Their sugars are slow to change to starch. They are, however, more sensitive to cold and disease. They will also cross-pollinate with any other sweet corn within 250 feet, so they must be grown carefully and well apart from other sweet corns. Two varieties we've grown to love are Honey 'N Pearl (bicolor), and Northern Xtra-Sweet yellow). We can expect to pay more for the "SUPERSWEETS" when they're available at roadside markets.

Corn problems are usually one of these three. Lodging—stalks fall over after a stiff wind. Protect stalks by hilling around them when you go out to hoe. Insects—corn earworms and corn borers are the main culprits. Earworms are the little caterpillars that crawl into the tips of the ears and chew away. Spraying/dusting with bacillus thuriengiensis will take care of them. Or we can put up with them and just cut off the damaged end when harvesting. Borers are another bigger problem. These flesh-colored caterpillars drill into leaves, stalks and ears—they're not fussy. Again, Bt is the answer. As to prevention, be sure to get old plants out of your garden site in the fall so the borers have no place to call their winter hideaway. Four-legged critters—deer, raccoons and squirrels can wreck a fabulous corn harvest in just one night's work. And funny thing how they seem to know when the corn is the perfect ripeness! Deer require serious fencing since they can jump 8 feet. Hanging bars of soap, wads of dog/human hair, shiny objects, or spraying with repellents—these all may work for awhile, until the deer realize they are just for entertainment! I know of gardeners who have had success keeping animals away by playing loud radio music. Success was short-lived, though, when one night they could swear they saw the raccoons dancing! What does work? Electric fencing, and lots of it. Several strands at various levels are necessary to keep out raccoons. Squirrels are a nuisance, too. Paper bags over each ear will discourage them, but that can be a big chore, depending on the number of plants in your garden.

How much is too much when it comes to the price we'll pay to grow our own sweet corn? When a thumb scratch brings a white milky fluid oozing from a fresh kernel, and we quickly strip off the husks and silks and plunge the ear into hot water, and frost the ear with butter before taking that first bite a few minutes later, we'll swear that it was all worth it!

Weeds, weeds, they're all over in my yard. Broad-leaf weeds such as plantain and dandelions are having a hey day this summer. Patience is the answer. This isn't the time to reach for the spray bottle to kill them off. The empty spaces left will fill in quickly with annual weeds that will sprout practically overnight. Fall is a much better time to spray broadleaf weeds. Until then, the best thing to do is mow the lawn on a regular basis, but not any shorter than 2 1/2 inches, especially in hot weather. By mowing regularly, we won't take off more than a third of the total height at any one time. During dry spells, keep in mind that the best way to water is to really soak the grass well so the entire root system gets a good drink, and not to water again until the soil really dries out. If we water too frequently, the soil surface stays moist and weed seeds are encouraged to sprout. By the time September rolls around, I'll have more time to fuss with the yard and do some serious spot spraying of weeds.

Did you know that the dog days of summer have nothing to do with dogs on this earth, but rather dogs up in the sky? These days, often sultry and downright hot, are named for the star Sirius, which is part of the constellation Canis Major (the Greater Dog) that we can see in the early morning sky during the month of July. And to think my dogs believe the world revolves around them!

Keep your flowers, annuals and especially roses, deadheaded to encourage more blooms. And if you haven't already done so, set out a barrel or large pail under the down spout to collect rain water for plants. It's much tastier to our plants than the cold well water we often have to use.

THE DEPENDABLE DOZEN

Many of our favorite perennial flowers bloom in the spring. Peonies, irises, bleeding hearts, and geraniums top my list of early bloomers. But which perennials can we count on when it comes to late summer blossoms? Which flowers perk up during the heat of August and yet endure the cool evenings signaling that autumn is just around the corner? The following is a list of suggestions I have compiled from my kitchen window view.

Rudbeckia - (Goldsturm) commonly called brown-eyed Susan. This brilliant golden yellow daisy outshines all other flowers in my small flower garden. Every morning I look for its glow as the sun creeps over the horizon (I'm an early riser). At maturity, Goldsturm reaches about 3 feet in height. This plant has been in my garden for three years and is already over three feet wide. Goldsturm is just as cheery in a vase on our dining room table as it is outdoors. It seems that the more I cut it for bouquets, the more it blossoms. I wouldn't be without this terrific perennial.

Echinacea - (Purple Coneflower) From a distance these pinkish-purple daisies look great although they're beginning to deteriorate by September. I try to keep all of my flowers dead-headed (old blooms cut off) to prevent energy going into seed production, but this flower is one exception. The large brown seed heads are stunning and the birds love them. In addition, I'm hoping they'll seed themselves and spread into nearby territory. The coneflower is a favorite of butterflies, which adds to their charm. As with Goldsturm, they are gorgeous in bouquets.

Monarda - (Bee Balm) There are so many names for this perennial flower but whatever the name, you won't be disappointed! This is also a perennial of many colors and heights. Many of the newer varieties are more resistant to mildew, which can be a constant problem with Monarda. The variety called Blue Stocking, which is actually more purple than blue, is resistant to mildew, and blooms later in the summer. I received a clump of red Monarda from a friend two years ago and it is also a late bloomer. This is a "must" for a butterfly garden.

Hardy Shrub Roses - For the umpteenth time this summer, my newly planted Morden's Blush shrub rose is blooming. In fact, it's more accurate to say that it has never stopped! Two of my favorite roses from the Morden series from Canada are Blush and Centennial. Unlike the older varieties of shrub roses, these bloom throughout the summer. The Hansa shrub that I retrieved from our old farm is also blooming again. Before buying a shrub rose, be sure to check for bloom time on the attached tag, as bloom time varies from one shrub rose to another.

Liatris - (Gay Feather) This flower reminds me of a bottle brush with its spike of puffy flowers opening from the top down. Most flowers open in the reverse, from the bottom up. Liatris is actually at its best during August. Mine are browning out rapidly now and are ready to be clipped off. They come in various heights from 3 to 6-foot stalks. The variety Kobold is a dwarf variety 2 feet tall with bright purple blooms. Most liatris blooms are purple, pink or white.

Eupatorium - (Joe Pye Weed) I confess to not having this in my garden for lack of space, but it's definitely on my list of favorites anyway! In fact, if you watch the roadside ditches for patches of purple this time of year, in all likelihood those are the wild version of Joe Pye. Eupatorium likes moist soil, hence the appearance of Joe Pye in the swampy ditches, and naturalizes easily. According to my perennial book, some varieties can reach 10 feet. It goes without saying that this perennial belongs in the back of our flower gardens!

Echinops - (Globe Thistle) I like this perennial for the interesting texture and shape it adds to our gardens. Yes, it does indeed look like a thistle! The leaves are spiny and course, and the globular flowers are bristly as well. They make terrific dried flowers for bouquets and are usually in shades of blue.

Hemerocallis - (Day Lilies) These marvelous flowers offer a wide choice of plant sizes, flower colors and periods of bloom. Some varieties bloom early in the summer while others continue to bloom later on, almost into fall. Be sure to know what you're buying when you select the day lily for your garden. They are truly hardy for our area, can be transplanted at almost any time of the year although early spring is the best time, and thrive in full sun to partial shade. The more shade, the less flowers.

Solidago - (Goldenrod.) These are perfect for informal gardens. They prefer full sun and well-drained soil and grow anywhere from 18 inches to 6 feet in height depending on the variety. Goldenrods are bright and feathery in fall bouquets and retain their color well when dried.

Sedum - (Autumn Joy) There are many varieties of sedums, but one that becomes spectacular once fall arrives is Autumn Joy. Late in summer it develops rosy pink flower buds that form above its graying green fleshy leaves. In the fall these buds open to a bronze-red which, if left in place over winter, turn to a golden brown. Autumn Joy is a tough plant that thrives in the full sun. It will gradually spread without becoming invasive.

Phlox - Depending on the weather/season, growing site and variety, phlox flowers all summer long. It usually will bloom longer if sheltered from the hot afternoon sun. The important thing to keep in mind about planting phlox is that it needs a lot of air circulation to help prevent mildew. Give them lots of room and plant them where they'll bask in the breezes.

Chrysanthemum - (Mums) There's a reason that mums are the last on my list. Although they come into their glory this time of year, they aren't always hardy for our area. I planted two last fall and only one survived. By the way, it's a lovely mound of bronze color and I'm hoping it will make it through the winter once again. Florist chrysanthemums are lovely as indoor plants, but don't think for a minute that they'll survive outdoors up here. The hardiest mums are those developed by the University of Minnesota but they aren't always easy to find in our garden centers. The series called "My Favorite" mums is a recent development of the University and is sold by the Ball Company. Ask for these at your local garden center. Maybe the best way to be sure of a truly hardy mum is to get a division from a friend who has an up-north-survivor mum.

HOSTA LA VISTA BABY

Say "hello" to hosta if you want it made in the shade! Here's a shade-loving plant that will fill in that empty space along the north side of your house, or follow the curve along the path to your front door. By the time August rolls around, clumps of hostas with their large, luxuriant leaves are sending up stick-like stems that are ready to blossom all along their length. Take notice of these lovely shade lilies. They may be just what you're looking for. If it's razzle dazzle color that you prefer, hostas might bore you. On the other hand, you may find that they're a refreshing, cool contrast under the warm August sun.

Through the years we gardeners develop a skepticism toward any plant that's called "carefree" or "foolproof." Who do they think they're kidding? We weren't born yesterday! But here's a plant that makes me eat those words. Hostas are as long-lasting as they are lovely. They're survivors. Up here in the northland, that's really saying a mouthful. They're pest-free except for the occasional slug that likes to hide beneath the huge leaves. Hostas aren't fussy about soil and thrive in the sun as well as the shade in the north where the summers are relatively cool. What more could we ask?

As you've already figured out, hostas are grown primarily for their foliage. Many of their flowers are rather insignificant compared to the glorious leaves, although some varieties have heavily scented blooms. Foliage comes in every shade of green imaginable from blue-green to chartreuse to almost gold. I have two variegated hostas with smaller green leaves streaked with white. They are lovely accent plants and their foliage is attractive in flower arrangements.

Hostas come in an assortment of sizes. Blue Angel with its platter-size leaves reaches four feet whereas Thumb Nail is only two inches high. Aureo Marginata, one of the most special (and expensive!) hostas from Japan, with large green leaves margined in yellow, grows two feet tall and a yard wide. It lists in garden catalogs for $28, which means it won't find its way into my garden anytime soon, but it must be a true prize!

Some hosta leaves are smooth and waxy; others are ribbed or puckered like seersucker. They create a lovely contrast in texture and color when combined with ferns. The great variety of sizes, shapes and colors in the hosta family makes them helpful in solving landscape problems. The thick leaf cover of mature plants smothers weeds, so they are excellent ground covers. They even fit in on stony slopes and help hold soil in place with their extensive root system.

The hosta variety we choose depends on the way we want to use it. Hostas for the background should be larger varieties. Some hostas are so splendid that they can be used alone as specimen plants. Some of the variegated kinds appear at their best in light shade although they'll do well in full sun, too. Those with blue foliage get their best color in the shade. Hostas will grow in ordinary garden soil, but if we give them ample moisture and organic matter such as peat moss, compost or well-rotted manure, they'll form the most luxuriant clumps.

They are best started as divisions, small plants made by dividing a large, vigorous clump. Fall is a fine time for dividing older clumps or setting out new plants. Give them some protection from winter's harshness this first year by covering them with a light mulch once the ground has frozen. Don't mulch in this manner too early or mice may set up housekeeping and make a few meals out of the tasty hosta roots. Hostas are especially attractive when surrounded with mulches such as cocoa beans, pine needles or wood chips. These mulches can be added anytime to help keep down weeds. Slugs love soft mulches, so if they become a problem in your hosta beds, you may have to go easy on the decorative mulches. Slugs are crafty critters. Any hiding spot for a slug snooze needs to be eliminated. Time will tell you whether they'll be a problem. Water hostas during dry spells from underneath the leaves. An overhead pounding by water sprinklers sometimes can damage the leaves in a manner similar to hail storms. Water early in the day so there's a better chance that the area will dry out before evening and slug-cruising time.

Autumn

Autumn ❧

The morning that Dad switched from his straw hat to his cloth cap with the Farmers' Union logo signaled the end of summer on the farm. It usually happened well into September, about the time that geese far overhead were veeing their way south, and the first of the field mouse invaders was snapped in the trap by the basement door. We kids were in too much of a hurry to catch the school bus to notice the change, although we were well aware of the swarms of flies congregating on the screen door and the tantalizing aroma of pot roast and apple crisp baking in the oven when we stumbled through this same door in the late afternoon. Mom has always been a terrific cook, enhancing escalloped potatoes from the garden with heavy cream from the milk cows, and adding freshly-picked peas for a truly heavenly eating experience. Nothing went to waste from her garden, or from the farm, for that matter. We used up everything. Clothes that couldn't be handed down any longer were crammed into the rag bag. Manure was spread onto the fields and the garden. Dinner left-overs were eaten at suppertime, and bones plus other available goodies were put into the dog dish. Chickens were adept at eating anything, including their own eggs if we weren't on time to collect them, and true to form, the pigs savored all of the potato peelings and vegetable trimmings. Plastic garbage bags weren't needed during this era of self-sufficiency. What we threw away ended up in the woods behind the barn.

A special fall day for me when I was a grade-schooler was the day that the crew came to fill the silo. Dad always planted a few fields of corn for just this purpose, but he needed help to bring it in to the silo where the chopped corn would ferment into nutrient-rich cattle food. I would always run the entire length of the driveway after school, hoping to get in on as much excitement as possible. Men would be hurrying around by the barn, some driving the trucks laden with chopped corn, others manning the elevator that transported it up into the temporary silo made of fencing lined with tarps. It was noisy and smelly, and I loved it! Mom cooked and washed dishes all day long, serving up meals fit for kings. This was all part of the process of getting ready for the long winter ahead. Cattle needed food; our family needed food. The silo was eventually filled and the basement pantry was lined with canned beans, tomatoes, pickles, peaches and apples. Winter squash and red potatoes awaited their turn on the cool basement floor. Did we have enough to last the winter? Better to have too much than not enough. Was it soon time to pile straw bales around the house to keep it snug and cozy during the big freeze? We not only mulched the rose bush; we mulched the house as well. It was almost time for the winter slow-down when we all hibernated beneath layers of snow and frost. Only time could tell if we had made adequate provisions to last until spring's revival. But the assurance from previous years of planning gave us the confidence to know when to quit storing up and when to put the extra log on the fire. If I listen closely I can still hear the chirping crickets.

MULTIPLY PERENNIALS BY DIVIDING

Sharpen your spade, slap on some sunscreen, and come along with me—it's time to divide perennial flowers. The contest between perennial and annual flowers—which are best?—is a discussion often heard between gardeners. Neither one loses. But one plus on the perennial side is that one plant, if it survives our harsh winters, will soon be large enough to become at least two or three more. This ability to produce is a lure that many of us don't want to pass up!

When is the best time of year to divide our perennial flowers? The general rule of thumb goes like this: plants that flower early in the spring such as peonies and irises are best divided in the late summer/early fall when they are snoozing. This is their dormant time. On the other hand, plants that flower in mid to late summer tolerate division in the early spring. Let's not forget the rule of thumb, on the other hand, that says to divide plants when we have the time to do so! The main thing to remember is this: don't divide plants in the middle of the hot summer, or right in the middle of their blooming time when they're sending all their energy into flower growth. Some plants are so tough and resilient that they don't mind being divided spring or fall. Included in this group are my favorites: daylilies, hostas, Veronica, rudbeckia, coneflowers, phlox, liatris, sedum and yarrow.

How do we tell if a plant needs to be divided? By looking! If a plant has a nice shape, blooms with a flourish, and fits well in the spot where it was planted, then leave well enough alone! If it sprawls all over, has crept well beyond its boundaries where you planted it, and isn't blooming as luxuriantly as it has in the past, then it will benefit from dividing. Many garden books advise us to be ready to divide perennials every 2 to 5 years. I think we gardeners will be the judge. Rather than counting calendar years, I'll count on my own eyesight and intuition.

What do we need in our dividing arsenal? Most important is a sharp spade. A garden fork or pitch fork comes in handy, along with a tarp or piece of heavy-duty plastic on which to place the division while we're practicing our surgery. Another strong person is always good to have around, especially if they're on the receiving end of extra plant divisions. Incentive works! A pail for water or a watering hose nearby is important once the divisions have been replanted. This list is short, which makes it easily remembered. There's no confusing it with our weekly grocery list.

How to begin? Here's my how-to from when I divided three clumps of daylilies. Dear friends who are leaving the area gave me the green light to dig up some daylilies before they put their house on the selling market. Always with my hand out for these valuable plants, I tossed my spade and fork into the back seat and drove into their yard early one morning. After removing all the dried leaves left over from last season, I took my spade with the deepest blade and cut a circle around the entire clump, being careful to give the roots wide berth. It's better to have more roots and soil than not enough. And there's no reattaching roots once the spade has gotten too close! Elmer's glue can do a lot in this world, but that's not one of them! A good 6 to 8 inches away from the base of the plants is a minimal amount. We can always shake off excess dirt later.

Once I had carved my way all around the clump, I stuck my sturdiest spade into the cut and pulled the handle back and forth to loosen it. I jiggled and pried the plant from all directions until it felt loose enough to lift from the ground. Then, summoning all my energies, I once again inserted my large spade and pulled the handle back toward me, lifting the clump from the ground. Once it was out and lying on its side, I took my spade and gave it a good thwack to break it into two large pieces. Daylilies have fibrous rootballs that sometimes require several such barbaric jabs. In fact, a small handsaw is sometimes needed to help cut through the mass of roots that have accumulated through the years. Small clumpers like columbines and primroses can be pried apart by hand, but we need to resort to more brutal measures with huge stubborn clumpers such as hostas, astilbes and daylilies.

The size and number of divisions from the plant depends on the size of the parent plant, the garden space where you intend to replant, and the number of friends who also want a piece! Pieces that are too small will take a longer time to reestablish themselves. We usually want pieces that are big enough to get growing again quickly, but that are small enough not to require dividing again in a few years. It's really a matter of personal needs and tastes.

As to replanting, get the divisions back into the soil as soon as possible without letting the roots dry out. Doing this dirty work beneath a cloudy, even a rainy sky, is the best since it means less exposure to the sun. We all wilt quickly when the sun is high. Trimming back the foliage to get it in the same proportion as the roots is also a good way to help minimize water loss through transpiration. Always plant the divisions at the same depth as they were originally planted. Keep them well watered for the first weeks of growth, and shield them from the bright sun until they are accustomed to their new home.

It's always a good idea to mulch these newly divided perennials in the late fall to help them get through their first winter. Although this idea of pampering goes against my grain, I'm willing to provide a little tender loving care initially as these plants become acclimated to our severe weather. After a year of good living, they're on their own!

MUM'S THE WORD

When it comes to planting a perennial in our flower gardens that is perfect for glorious fall color, choose chrysanthemums. "Mums" come in a wide variety of flower colors from whites and creams to lemon and golden yellows and on to apricots, oranges, mauves, roses, reds and burgundies. The only color non-existent in the mum world is blue, but hybridizers are likely working on it right this minute. Chrysanthemums in their bright autumn colors are spectacular, especially when grouped around other fall beauties such as asters, sedum and rudbeckia.

Mums are favored as garden flowers for their brilliance both IN the garden and OUT. They make excellent cut flowers, retaining their colors and perkiness in bouquets for days on end. My main complaints about mums have to do with their borderline hardiness when left without mulch and the lateness in the season that they are available to us gardeners for planting. Most of the time they show up at garden centers in the late summer, when in reality they have a much better chance of surviving our harsh winters if we get them in the ground early. Late plantings mean less time for them to establish tough root systems which support them in the cold weather, much like our addition of a layer of insulating fat that begins to accumulate with a hearty Thanksgiving feast! Let's ask our local nurseries to bring them in earlier if possible.

Three basic rules determine our success with mums: appropriate variety for our northern area, a sunny, well-drained planting site, and winter protection. Normally I scratch any perennials from my list that require the extra pampering of winter mulch. But in special cases such as mums, Russian sage and oriental lilies, I'm willing to forego my earlier oath and pile on the straw, evergreen branches and pine needles once the ground has frozen.

Garden chrysanthemums aren't terribly fussy about soils except for one thing: good drainage. Nothing will kill off a mum faster than sitting in wet soil. If your soil is heavy with clay, add lots of humus, peat moss and well-rotted manure before planting. It's also a good idea to add a complete fertilizer (5-10-10) at the same time because mums are heavy eaters. Select a planting site where the mum will get an abundance of sunshine. Plants in semi-shady locations will be taller, have weaker stems that may break off, and will bloom later in the fall. The root systems of mums are close to the surface of the soil. which means they react quickly to dry spells. Keep them watered with 1to 2 inches of moisture weekly.

Which variety is best for our area? Since mums vary so widely in cold hardiness, I'll take chances only with the cultivars developed at the University of Minnesota. Years of plant breeding where they've been selected for superior flower characteristics, growth habits and hardiness has produced a long list of possibilities. Most of these cultivars are early blooming, which assures flowers before a killing frost in our area. The problem with late blooming cultivars is that they may not bloom early enough to escape the clutches of Ol' Jack. A partial list of varieties includes: the Minn-series (Minnglow, Minnpink, Minnruby, etc) which are mostly low-growing mid-season bloomers; Centerpiece, Dr. Longley, Golden Star, Lemonsota, and Maroon Pride. Look also for the "My Favorite" series of mums sold by the Ball company. Last year I found them in the garden section of our local Home Depot.

Florist mums are in another category altogether. These attractive potted plants, usually available all year long, make terrific house plants and can be cut back to 3 to 4 inches in the spring and planted in the garden. Don't expect them to winter over. They may green up nicely, but take such a long time to bloom outdoors that they likely won't beat the frost. Even with plenty of mulch, they usually won't make it through the winter.

Mums succumb to insect and disease problems just like any other garden flower, but if we keep these points in mind, we can avoid most: buy healthy, pest-free plants; plant in a sunny spot; allow plenty of air circulation by not overcrowding plants; keep weeds which harbor pests and diseases away from plants.

Mums have traditionally required "pinching" to keep their compact shape and not become leggy. Newer cultivars maintain their shape without this ritual, but if you have older varieties in your gardens, you've likely found that careful nipping back the tips in the early growing season produces more branching and stockier plants. Stop this pinching process by July or you may end up taking off the flower buds.

How many times have you heard me preach about the importance of dead-heading flowers, both annuals and perennials? It's almost a mantra among us gardeners. Clip, clip, clip off those dead flowers so the plant's energy doesn't go into the seed. There are some perennials that have attractive seed heads that will enhance our gardens in the fall and winter and provide seeds for our bird friends. Consider leaving the seeds on the astilbe, sedum (Autumn Joy), echinacea (purple coneflower), perovskia (Russian sage), allium (flowering onion), echinops (globe thistle), papaver (poppy), solidago (goldenrod), Siberian iris, and rudbeckia (yellow coneflower).

Fall is an extraordinary time in our northern gardens where we can see the dramatic change of seasons. The light is usually clear but low, which casts a glow over the changing foliage color of trees, shrubs and perennials. Flower colors take on a depth and brilliance that's almost washed out under the hot, direct summer sun. This is the perfect time to haul out our cameras and snap photos of our gardens as reminders of the beauty of our gardening world during the winter.

INNOCENT GOLDENROD - GUILTY RAGWEED

Aaaachoo! Think you're coming down with a late summer cold? Itchy weeping eyes, stuffy nose and sneezing from dawn to dusk might not indicate a cold, but hay fever. Bright yellow goldenrod often gets the blame. Roadsides and open fields are dotted with their showy yellow spikes and we're quick to conclude that their pollen must be the reason for our symptoms. But goldenrod is truly innocent. The real culprit is ragweed.

Ragweed normally grows anywhere from one to five feet tall and is found all over in late summer in roadside ditches, along fence lines and at the edges of our gardens. As I was driving into our lane yesterday, I slowed down to a crawl, rolled down the car window, and saw patches of them springing up through the gravel and clinging to the roadside edge. Here's a job for my tractor mower once it gets out of the repair shop. Unlike the flamboyant goldenrod, ragweed has small, unremarkable green flowers that unleash gigantic amounts of sneeze-causing pollen.

There are 15 species of ragweed, but the three we find in our area are common, western and giant. Judging by the growth habit of the plants by our driveway, I'd guess they are of the "common" variety. This is an annual that reproduces from seeds with a shallow root and grayish, deeply lobed foliage.

Goldenrod has been given a bad rap. To some of us it's a roadside weed. To others it's a medicinal herb and to still others, it's a treasured garden flower. Of the 130 goldenrod species, at least 45 are found in Minnesota alone. The gray goldenrod (*solidago nemoralis*) is the most common in our area. The genus name, SOLIDAGO, is from the Latin *solida* meaning "whole" and *ago* meaning "to make," a name given to goldenrod which has long been associated with wound healing. Native Americans used the roots to heal burns, treated fevers and snakebite with tea made from crushed flowers, and chewed roots to soothe sore throats. According to Rodale's book on herbs, modern medicine offers no evidence that it's an effective medicine, but neither are any serious illnesses or medical problems connected with the plant. If you have a lot of allergies, especially to pollens, it would be wise to stay clear of it.

While most Minnesotans likely think of goldenrod as nothing but roadside weeds, it is a popular, yes, even truly admired addition to European flower gardens. Does that surprise you? The horticultural varieties of goldenrod are moving toward larger flower heads and shorter stems, which makes them a terrific border plant. Since they thrive in poor soil, we should sit up and take notice! In rich soil they tend to grow too tall and topple over. *Milaegers Gardens* lists the variety "Peter Pan" under Solidago. Hardy in zones 3 to10, it's listed as easy to grow in sun or light shade, great for fall color, not fussy about soil, and reaches a height of 2 feet.

Goldenrod is lovely in bouquets, both as a fresh flower and in dried arrangements. Although they don't dry as bright as their fresh color, they do retain a nice golden hue and are a perfect addition to fall centerpieces and displays. Since I haven't any tame varieties growing in my gardens, I plan to stroll down our drive and cut a few of these lovely "weeds".

Warm days lately are welcome ones. Maybe there's still hope for my green tomatoes. Several more sunny days like today will boost them along. Tomatoes always develop the best flavor when we let them ripen on the vine, but sometimes this isn't possible. If we have to pick them early, they'll have the best flavor and ripen evenly when left at room temperature. Don't put them on the windowsill in the sunlight or in the refrigerator. The bottom canopy of leaves on my tomato plants is yellowing/browning out quickly, but this time of year that isn't a problem. In fact, a few less leaves will hasten the ripening of the fruits. Two plants are so heavy with tomatoes and are leaning so heavily to one side that they've pulled the cage right out of the ground. Here's where the advantage of planting in raised beds is obvious—the tomatoes are still way up in the air.

I paid a quick visit to the local Farmers' Market this morning and was pleasantly surprised to see such a nice variety of vegetables, all in perfect eating condition. Green beans with just a wee bit of bean bulging the pods, cukes in all shapes and sizes, small red potatoes perfect for topping with peas in cream sauce, and slender zucchini that will be tasty in our favorite meatball stew recipe. Stop by for home-grown produce if your garden is small like mine. The pails of freshly-cut gladiolas were gorgeous. I couldn't resist the huge spikes of some lovely pink glads which are now presiding over our dining room table. New choices of vegetables, fruits, plants and flowers appear weekly. Stop by and take a look.

TEN TIMELY TIPS FOR FALL

A gardener's work is never done! Springtime finds us overwhelmed with tilling, planting, seeding, fertilizing, pruning, spading, and so on. Fall seems equally as busy. We're all in a hurry to harvest our crops before Jack Frost pays us an unwelcome visit. Plus we all know that winter will be upon us before we care to know about it! That means lots of tasks ahead in preparation for the white season. To help us list priorities for fall, I've come up with ten that I think need our attention.

DON'T fertilize shrubs and trees this time of year. In fact, put that box of fertilizer away for the season so it won't be tempting (much like that chocolate candy bar in the freezer!). Trees and shrubs need time to prepare for winter, too. Gradually as the days and nights cool down, their branches begin to "harden off" so they won't be killed by the cold temperatures. A shot of fertilizer this time of year will encourage fresh growth which surely won't harden off in time to live through the winter. Water shrubs well, especially those newly planted, if we happen to have a dry spell before snow comes. But keep your hands off that fertilizer box.

DON'T even think of quitting lawn mowing yet! If it's green and growing, we have to keep mowing it. I know, I'm getting tired of the job myself. Many of us have been at it since the end of April. That makes almost 6 months of waiting for a sunny day when the grass isn't soaked with rain. Think of it this way. Mowing is easier than shoveling! Remember that lawns benefit from the grass clippings that fall back on it. According to the University of Minnesota Extension, these clippings contain nutrients that are good for the lawns. They don't build up thatch. Speaking of thatch, fall is a good time to rent a thatching machine if the thatch buildup is well over half an inch. Some thatch is good. It acts as a cushion and protects grass roots. Too much, on the other hand, suffocates the roots, doesn't allow for good absorption of fertilizers and water, and needs to be taken off. Take a sharp knife, cut a small block of sod from your yard, and check the thatch level. Then you'll know for sure. Anything over 1/2 inch requires our attention.

DON'T bring houseplants that have been summering outdoors back inside without checking them over well. Some plants have a natural tendency to attract pests. Impatiens and fuchsias are two of these culprits. They always (well, almost always!) have spider mites. Others, such as geraniums, rarely have pests attached. Apparently they taste awful. What to do? Give your plants a bath with an insecticidal soap available at garden centers and many hardware stores. Sometimes a stronger insecticide may be needed, as in the case of mealy bugs. If possible, set these plants aside in a separate room from your other houseplants for a couple of weeks. This will give you time to make sure they are de-bugged before returning them to your healthy plant neighborhood.

DON'T wait until the ground freezes hard before planting spring flowering bulbs. Daffodils and crocus need time this fall to send down some roots and get acclimated before winter sets in. Add some all-purpose bulb food around the bottom of the bulbs for good eating come spring. As for tulips, they don't need as much time in the ground and can almost be planted after a snowfall! October is a good time to put them in the ground. If you're buying new bulbs this fall, pay attention to the time of bloom. There are early, mid-season, and late-blooming tulips. Plant some of each for the best show.

DON'T forget that fall is the best season for planting shrubs, provided we don't dilly-dally too long.

Shrubs are often on special sale this time of year because garden centers don't want to have them hanging around in their often too-small greenhouses over winter. Water these newly-planted shrubs well but don't do any pruning which will trigger new growth.

Enough of the DON'Ts. How about the DOs?

DO rake leaves once they have fallen, especially those beneath fruit trees and any other trees that have had badly diseased leaves. Diseased leaves left on the ground may re-infest the tree next year. It isn't a good idea to use these raked leaves as mulch, either, for the same reason. Compost them, or bag them up for the community compost pile. Composting should kill off the disease-causing microbes.

DO empty out all containers that held flowers and vegetables, and be ready to start over with fresh soil next season. The soil that has nourished our container plants has no vigor left (don't we gardeners know the feeling?) and will be useless for future plants. Instead, put it on your garden plot where it will mix in with the rest of the dirt.

DO cut back peonies and irises this time of year. Both of these perennial flowers are susceptible to disease which can find a snug home in the plant leaves if we don't cut them off. Cut peony leaves off (plus stems) right at or even slightly below ground level. Irises needn't be given such a shearing. Cut them down to about 4 to 6 inches. Discard all of these plant materials; don't let them fall back on the soil around the plants.

DO fertilize your lawn a couple of times this fall before the snow flies. Fall is the best time to give our lawns nourishment. Perennial grasses are soaking up nutrients this time of year and sending them down to their roots so they can make it through winter and stay alive. An application in September and one again in mid-October is the best time for lawn fertilizers. Water it in well if there isn't rain, and make sure fertilizer doesn't end up on your sidewalk or driveway. For this reason, a drop spreader is often considered better than a broadcast spreader that whirls the fertilizer in many directions. If fertilizer does get on your drive or sidewalk, sweep it up and put it back on the lawn where it will soak into the soil and not end up in our lakes and streams.

DO take a soil test once you've cleaned up your garden spot. It's easy and doesn't hurt! What's more, it will help you make the best decisions next year when it comes to improving your soil and, when all's said and done, getting the most healthy plants. Pick up a soil test kit at your local Extension Office Then follow the included directions. This test will tell you the amount of humus in your soil, and also the pH level (acid versus alkaline). If you have both flower gardens and vegetable gardens, you'll want to have both areas tested.

BRING IN TENDER BULBS AND GREEN TOMATOES

Jack Frost came within a hair's-breadth of nabbing us in his icy grip last week. I raced for the window thermometer while struggling into my cozy sweatshirt, a mere 34 degrees outside! That's close! There are too many fruits still ripening on the vine, too many flowers blooming their hearts out, to lose them overnight to Jack's capricious whim. But his visit shouldn't be that unexpected. With one ear tuned to the forecast and a stack of old sheets and rugs by the door, we can prolong our gardening season for a few days.

There's no question that tomatoes taste best when they're ripened on the vine. But with Jack lurking around, this might not be possible. If I get tired of covering plants overnight and uncovering them by day, I may just give up and pick tomatoes instead. Those that have already turned light green will ripen easily indoors. Any that are deep green and hard as rocks won't be as flavorful so maybe I'll chop these up, add onions and peppers, and make a sauce for sandwiches and meats (although I don't RELISH the thought!).

Believe it or not, tomatoes DON'T ripen best on a sunny windowsill. Keep them out of direct sunlight, at temperatures around 60 to 70 degrees. If we ripen them in a cool basement, the flavor won't be as good. It sometimes helps to wrap tomatoes separately in tissue or newspaper when storing many at a time. That way they don't touch each other, and decay is not spread so easily from one to another. If I have time, I will dip them in a pail of water to which I've added a tablespoon of disinfectant. This seems to cut down on decay. Be sure to rinse and dry them off well before packing them away. Storing anything wet is asking for trouble.

I've heard of gardeners who have successfully ripened tomatoes by pulling out the entire plants and hanging them indoors where it's warm but not sunny. Since I've never tried this, I can't say much about it other than it's important to remove fruit as soon as it ripens, and also to take off any fruit that is starting to spoil.

We'll need to think about taking in tender bulbs soon. Tender bulbs are those that can't withstand our winters. They remind me of some of our friends who need to winter in Texas and Arizona. Dahlias, glads, cannas, tuberous begonias and caladiums would be happier in these southern states, too. But it would be expensive to rent them a condo, so we'll have to buy some vermiculite (sand will also do the job, as will wood shavings) and dig them up carefully this fall so they don't spend the winter outdoors.

Tuberous begonias should be brought indoors before a hard frost. Dig up the entire plants with some soil attached and put them in a warm place to dry off. Remove the leaves when they have dried up, clean off the tubers and store them in a box of vermiculite, wood shavings or sphagnum moss at around 50 to 60 degrees. I plan to winter my hanging basket of red begonias right in the container. By the looks of it, they're getting ready to drop leaves any day now. I'll bring the basket into the warm garage until most of the plant has dried; then I'll store it downstairs in a large, brown grocery bag. Come spring, I'll soak it for 24 hours in warm water, pot and all, and then bring it out into more light and watch for the tubers to sprout.

Cannas are a bit hardier. After a killing frost has blackened the stems, cut them off at ground level, lift them carefully from the soil and let them dry indoors for a couple of weeks. Then store them in a dry material and keep them dark and cool. Cannas store best at temps between 40 to 50 degrees. I have trouble finding such a place in my house. Central heating may be perfect for people, but it's trouble for tubers, rhizomes and bulbs that like cool corners.

Cut dahlias down to about 6 inches after a frost. Dig them carefully and remove the clumps of soil clinging to the roots. Let them dry for a few days out of the sun and store them in vermiculite or sawdust. Here's the clincher. Dahlias need cool storage (35 to 45 degrees). My bedroom back on the old farm would have been ideal. That oil stove in the middle of the living room never cranked out enough heat to reach those corners in the middle of winter. Dahlias and cannas would have huddled together and been happy as clams in that old, cold house. A root cellar is the answer to our modern living.

I usually wait until we've had a few frosts before digging my glads, although if I went by the book I'd lift them earlier. Cut the tops off to 1/2 inch above the corms and destroy them. Don't add the tops to your compost pile, as too often glad foliage contains diseases that probably won't be killed off. Glads need to be dried rapidly. Put them on shallow trays in a warm, well-ventilated area and dry them for 2 to 4 weeks. Toward the end of this time, clean the corms by removing the dried parent corms and old roots. They'll usually just break off from the new corm. Sort through the corms and toss out any that aren't looking healthy and plump. Dust them with a fungicide/insecticide or a product called "bulb dust" and put them in paper bags. Plastic bags hold in moisture and bulbs stored in them will likely develop mold and decay. Ideally they should be stored at 40 to 45 degrees, although I have had luck keeping them in my basement, which is closer to 55 to 60. Remember to label bulbs if you are storing several varieties. Our memories may be good this week, but by next spring we'll have forgotten the contents without a label to remind us.

BRIGHT IDEAS ABOUT BULBS

Thoughts of spring are far away from our minds in fall. But this is the time to start planting those spring bulbs that revive us from the winter blahs and promise us that spring and summer days aren't far away.

Bulbs are those unique plants that endure unfavorable weather by living underground for more than half of their lives. To keep it simple, we're going to divide them into two categories: winter hardy types that bloom in spring and spring planted types that bloom in summer. Botanically speaking, some of these "bulbs" aren't truly bulbs. They may be corms (glads and crocuses), tubers (potatoes and anemones), or rhizomes (irises and lilies-of-the-valley). This doesn't really matter to us. We're more interested in what to choose that will survive up here, and when, where and how to plant them. The common winter-hardy bulbs that most of us will be planting this fall are tulips, narcissus (commonly called daffodils), crocuses, muscari (grape hyacinths), and hyacinths.

It isn't quite true that bulbs will bloom regardless of how or where we plant them. True, they are quite easily grown, but we can improve our success by remembering to do a few things first.

Buy good bulbs. The best place we can do this is at our local nurseries where we can actually examine the bulbs. You may have to order from a catalog if you want extra-special varieties, but for the more common bulbs, buy locally. Check for bulbs that are plump, firm and heavy (much like buying oranges and grapefruit) and without bruises, spots, green shoots, or shriveled areas. Generally speaking, the larger the bulb, the larger the flower. If they have on their dust covers (tunics), so much the better because these protect the bulbs from bruising and drying out.

Prepare your soil ahead of time. Add organic matter like decomposed leaves, peat moss and old compost from your pile out back. Don't add manure unless it's absolutely decomposed to the point that it's black dirt. Manure can burn bulbs and cause them to rot underground. Buy some bulb fertilizer if you don't already have some in your garden cupboard. Work it into the root zone of the bulbs according to directions. If you just sprinkle it on the surface, it will take a long time for it to reach the roots where it is needed.

Have a plan. Any kind of plan no matter how plain or elaborate. This way you'll know how many bulbs you need, what heights are best, and the colors you want that will blend well together. Bulbs planted in semi-shade will grow taller, emerge later, and last longer. Some, like the crocus, need the warmth of the sun to open. A bed of tulips on a southern slope or in the SW corner along your house will bloom earlier than one set out in the middle of your yard. Plant bulbs in groups of the same variety for the most visual impact. It's best to have at least 12 large bulbs together. Twenty to 25 smaller ones make a good-sized grouping.

When do we start planting? Any day now for several varieties. Lilies should be in the ground already. They need plenty of time to set down roots before the cold weather comes. Daffodils and grape hyacinths can go into the ground in September. Wait until late October to set out tulips.

There are two general planting methods. If you are planting a large bed, you might find it easiest to dig a trench for the bulbs. This way you'll plant bulbs of the same variety exactly the same depth and they will bloom at the same time. If you have something smaller in mind, just dig individual holes, either with a trowel or a bulb planter, which is a cone-shaped device that you push down into the soil to make the hole. How deep do you plant? The general rule of thumb is to plant bulbs at a depth equal to 3 times the diameter (widest part) of the bulb. The idea, especially in our frigid North, is to help the bulbs escape the terrible freeze. These bulbs are in a dormant state, but nonetheless they can freeze out if they aren't planted deep enough. If your soil is sandy like mine, plant a bit deeper. Plant the bulb with the growing tip UP. If you can't tell which end is up (I have days like that!), set the bulb in sideways. It will straighten itself out! Here are the distances for some common bulbs we'll be planting: tulips-6"deep, 4 to 6" apart; daffodils-6" deep, 6 to 8" apart; crocus-4"deep, 2 to 6" apart; muscari-(grape hyacinth) 2"deep, 2 to 4" apart; lilies-4 to 6" deep, 9 to 18" apart; iris rhizomes-just below the surface, 12" apart.

Water thoroughly after planting your bulbs. Then after the first heavy frost, give them a cozy blanket of clean straw to help ward off winter's chill. Don't be stingy. A thick covering of at least 6 to 8 inches will keep them snug until spring.

AUTUMN BRINGS A BITTERSWEET ENDING

Believe it or not, a successful gardening season for us begins, not in the spring as we often may think, but in the fall. Cleaning up our garden beds, tilling the soil to eliminate pests, taking a soil test, working in organic matter, and getting rid of surrounding weeds and refuse are all chores that will benefit us for the next growing season, as well as neaten up the place so we don't have to put up with a garden mess throughout the early winter. Eventually our bountiful snowfalls hide what we have left behind. What we take the time to do now will lessen our load next spring.

High on my list is a thorough tilling of my garden beds due to an uninvited guest this summer. Much to my chagrin, slugs found a happy home beneath huge summer squash leaves thriving in a raised bed. I about threw a tantrum one early morning when I saw one slide down a leaf stalk. By tilling that bed several times before snowfall, I'll bring them to the surface where they'll make a slippery snack for any hungry birds passing through. Shoot, I'll even set out some salsa if it will make them more palatable! One more word on slugs. At our State Master Gardeners' Conference I toured a 75-acre property that included a large hosta bed. The experienced owner/gardener covers his hosta plants every year with 3+ inches of pine needles. Come spring the hostas just pop up through the needles. Slugs don't like these needles, the hostas don't object to the acidy content of the needles, and everyone's happy.

Don't let Jack Frost get to your squash, pumpkins and gourds. While they may appear thick-skinned and able to withstand such chilly temps, actually they can't! If they aren't yet ripe, cover them with old rugs, blankets, or whatever you can find in the hall closet that you aren't wearing! How do you know if they're ripe? Give them the thumbnail test. Press the skin gently with your thumb nail. A ripe squash or pumpkin won't puncture easily. Obviously you don't want to test every one of your squash since they won't keep as well once they're punctured or bruised. Also look at the color. A ripe squash will lose some of its shininess and be more of a dull green. Once picked, they won't continue to ripen. Pumpkins, however, will still change colors and become orange after picking. They might not be good for cooking, but for jack-o-lanterns they'll be just fine.

Autumn evokes the same feelings as the name of a beautiful ornamental vine often found growing in the wild—bittersweet. Maybe you share this mixture of sadness and pleasure that I experience, watching the colorful leaves and gradual process that ends in a winter sleep for nature and our plants. The winter season is also a resting time for many of us northerners. Summer passes by in a flurry, full of chores, visiting friends and relatives, outings while the roads aren't slippery or snow-covered, grilling our favorite chicken recipe. The list is long and crammed with activity. Winter, on the other hand, offers us a time for reflection. No more mowing or weeding, no more pruning or fertilizing or spraying or harvesting. We can almost breathe a sigh of relief, and yet we know that about mid-winter we'll start feeling the juices rise and get the urge to once again plan our gardens for next year.

Before we forget about this season, let's remember to jot down some important notes. What did we try this year that didn't work well? Keep in mind that some summers, far from ideal for many of us gardeners, can be ideal for diseases and pests. What didn't work out one season may well thrive the next. Where did we plant that marguerite that was so lovely this summer? What is the name of that sunflower that we admired in a neighbor's garden? And where in the heck did we plant those lilies so we don't dig them up in the early spring? Now's the time to label, mark, photograph, and journal (if we didn't take time to do it before). My memory can't keep track from one year to the next. It needs the help I mentioned in order to function without my frustration level rising.

Speaking of bittersweet, one of these days I'm loading up my ladder and heading for my friend Cathy's yard. She has this hardy, deciduous vine climbing up a tree in her backyard, and some of its brightly colored berries are too high for easy picking. She has promised me some for fall decorations if I'll do the climbing to get them. Not being afraid of heights, I'm up to the challenge. American bittersweet (*Celastrus scandens*) is one of the most ornamental of our hardy northern vines. It is native to our area, and if we're lucky we can find it growing in thickets or along streams in our wooded areas. While we may appreciate it for its beauty, trees and shrubs aren't so enthusiastic because it can kill them off by tightly girdling their stems and branches.

Bittersweets aren't especially noticeable and put on little floral display except for their showiness in the autumn. It's in the fall that their clusters of yellowish-orange capsules separate, exposing bright red-orange berries. This usually happens in September. These berries remain attractive throughout the winter, which is the reason they are in demand for long-lasting decorations. I plan to trim a grapevine wreath with some of these berries and, depending on how high I climb, may have enough for a table centerpiece. Bittersweet vines grow well in most soils, in full sun or shade, but sunshine is needed for fruit production. The only care they need is an occasional pruning to keep them within bounds. Early spring is the best time for this chore. The trick to planting bittersweet is this: it needs both a male and female plant for fruit production. The two types must be near each other to produce fruit. In June, small greenish-white flowers open in clusters at the ends of branches. Bees are the main pollinators, although wind may also help out. We can buy plants from nurseries in the spring, or we can start our own from seeds or cuttings. Collect seeds from the fruits that have dried at room temperature for 2 to 3 weeks. Then remove seeds from the berries and let them dry for another week. In order to get good germination, these seeds must be stored in moist peat in a plastic bag/container, and kept cool in the refrigerator for 3 months. They will then be ready to be sown outdoors. How do we know if we have male or female plants? We don't! The only tell-tale signs are the blooms. The best way to get the sex ratio we want (1 male plant to 6 female plants) is to propagate plants from cuttings of the known sex.

To wrap up this season, keep these points in mind: wasps will die off with the cold weather. Don't worry about them anymore. Wrap thin-skinned trees (young maples and fruit trees especially) to prevent sun-scald. Trap pocket gophers and moles now because in the spring they produce litters. Get rid of mushrooms popping up in yards; these mushrooms are tempting to children and pets and are better off in our garbage bag. Prune large shade trees in early winter when they're dormant. Enclose azaleas and rhododendrons with chicken wire and fill in with leaves. They will protect the flower buds.

RETIRE ROSES AND PRUNE PEONIES

In spite of the beastly winters we northerners proudly endure, many gardeners successfully raise hybrid tea roses year to year. I puzzle over the reason they put themselves through such stress since these roses demand fussing and fuming, in addition to dusting and spraying. But the beauty of a hybrid tea rose can hardly be equaled, which I suspect is reason enough. If we purchase a healthy rose and get it planted in the early spring, most of us can have success for a few months and even see some lovely flowers. The true challenge is getting them to live through our winters. There are several ways we can attempt this great feat.

The styrofoam rose cones that begin raising their white beaks in stores this time of year offer us false hopes and not much else. While they may work for some locations and situations, they are probably the least reliable way of protecting plants through the cold season. In late winter and early spring as the sun begins to pick up strength, the insides of these cones heat up like small ovens. Instead of protecting the plant inside, they actually kill it off. What's left inside when we peek underneath the cone in the spring is a fried/steamed rose bush. That's a pitiful sight.

The "Minnesota tip" method of rose protection is definitely the most work but usually saves the majority of plants from year to year. Here's the process. Spray the rose with a fungicide/insecticide for roses. Tie the canes together to make the plant as compact as possible. Use something soft and pliable such as twine. If the rose has grown especially tall during the season, trim it back to about 1 1/2 feet. Dig a trench on one side of the bush that's at least a foot deep. Loosen the soil around the roots of the plant and then tip it into the trench. Cover the rose with soil taken from the trench and any extra that's available. Layer on a thick pile of straw, leaves or pine boughs. Mark the location of the rose base AND tip so you can dig it up next spring without causing it too much damage. This is an important step. Several years ago I trenched a couple of roses and by spring they were lost because my markers had blown down in the winter winds. Push those markers well into the ground!

Mounding rose bushes accomplishes the same thing as trenching but is less work. Cut each bush down to about 1 1/2 feet. Then mound soil over the entire bush. Don't skimp! Cover them with straw or leaves. This usually requires something to hold this mulch in place such as a circle of chicken wire or large pine boughs. In the spring when the ground begins to soften, gradually work the soil away from the stem until you're back to almost level ground. Whatever method you use, plan to protect your tender roses before night temps dip to 20 degrees.

Did all your peonies bloom last spring? If they developed buds that didn't open, they may be infected with a fungus called botrytis. This fall, cut plants all the way back to ground level or even just below the ground. I use a regular kitchen shears for this task. This will prevent the fungus from spending the winter on the peony foliage. As the plant shoots break through the soil next spring, spray the plant with a fungicide. You may need to spray several times during the spring if we have a lot of wet and cloudy days.

Sometimes we can avoid botrytis by taking some other kinds of action. Is the peony in full sun for most of the day? If it gets a lot of shade, you may need to move it to a sunnier spot, or do some tree trimming. Is the soil good or does it need more compost or peat moss mixed in?

Peonies also like high phosphorous fertilizer mixed into the soil in the early spring. Use a granular fertilizer and sprinkle it on the soil several inches away from the emerging shoots. Then carefully work the granules into the top inch or two of the soil. Moving a peony should be the last resort. They are like me and resist moving, or at least frown about it a lot. Try everything else first before hunting for your spade.

STORE THEM FRESH

Do you have fresh vegetables and fruits you hope to store over winter? There are three basic kinds of storage for fresh produce: warm and dry, cool and dry, and cool and moist. Once we decide which vegetables and fruits need what, we'll need to search for the best space available.

The first category, warm and dry, applies to pumpkins and winter squash. When we say "warm," we mean around 55 degrees. This is truly warm when compared to the other proper storage conditions. It's all relative, isn't it? Pumpkins and squash need to be kept dry and have some ventilation. Wipe off the dirt but don't scrub them down. Don't crowd them either. They need their space! A spare room in your house that's the last to receive heat from the furnace may work fine. Be sure to check on them from time to time to be sure they aren't deteriorating.

Cool and dry is perfect for onions. When the onion stems fall over, they are ready to be harvested because they won't continue growing at this point. "Cure" them in the sun alongside your garden (or in your heated garage) for a couple of weeks. Then dry them even more in a single layer on an old screen or some other material that allows good air flow. After a month of this drying out, they will be ready for storage. Net bags work well since they allow onions to stay dry. Never store them in plastic bags. Put the onions in an unheated closet or attic where they won't freeze.

Cool and moist is a real challenge. Lots of garden veggies like this category, but it isn't easy to find such a place in our modern homes. A root cellar that stays around 40 degrees is the ideal place for carrots, beets, rutabagas, turnips, potatoes, cabbages and apples. Those of us without root cellars have a problem and often have to resort to refrigerators. Carrots will keep for some time in plastic bags with holes punched in them. Potatoes like to be kept in the dark. They also like ventilation and less humidity to be in really good shape over a period of time. Sometimes the cement floor of a cool basement works out. Brush the dirt off potatoes before storage and be sure they don't freeze. Wherever we put them, we need to check on them and sort out those that are starting to spoil. There's nothing more stinky than a rotting potato! Carrots and beets store best at temps just above freezing. They will shrivel up if they are allowed to dry out, so keep them in heavy crocks covered with burlap or cloth. Leave at least 1/2 inch of top on beets or they'll bleed and dry out quickly.

It simply makes sense to store only ripe, healthy produce. Don't try to keep bruised apples, under-ripe squash or wormy onions. The end result will be a rotten, smelly mess in the bottom of our refrigerators or shelves. Any bruise or other opening in the skin of fruit or vegetables is an open door for bacteria and other invaders. Check your produce carefully. Eat anything that your spade or fork damaged and store only what's in tip-top shape.

Have you ever wondered what to do with all those pumpkin seeds after the traditional Halloween carving contest? Try roasting them. Wash the seeds thoroughly and discard any pulp. Let dry on a paper towel-lined cookie sheet. In a mixing bowl, mix seeds from 2 medium-sized pumpkins with 3 tablespoons olive oil. Spread onto cookie sheet and dust with salt. Bake at 350 degrees for 20 minutes or until seeds appear dry and darker in color. Watch so they don't get too dark. Serve them warm. For extra spice add 1 teaspoon each of cumin and chili powder when mixing seeds in the bowl. For a sweet snack use 2 teaspoons each nutmeg and sugar.

Don't let Jack Frost take a swipe at the decorative gourds in your garden or they will be damaged. Leave a couple inches of stem attached when harvesting gourds. This helps prevent disease organisms from entering the gourd and adds an interesting touch as the stem dries and curls. Wash newly harvested gourds in warm, soapy water; then rinse them in water with a few drops of household disinfectant. Dry them with a soft cloth and set them on several layers of newspaper in a sunny, warm location. Turn them now and then and in a week their color will be set and the skin toughened. Once again, wipe them with a cloth soaked in disinfectant solution. Store the gourds on newspapers in a warm, dark place for three weeks. This will help to dry them out and keep the colors from fading. If you prefer shiny gourds, give them a coat of shellac or varnish, or wax them with a paste floor wax. After all this, they'll be ready for your special harvest centerpiece.

CHORES FOR A LINGERING AUTUMN

It's a beautiful sight out my loft windows today. Perched up here above the living room I can watch the sun as it reaches the tops of the nearby birch trees, turning them into beacons of gold. Autumn is my favorite season of the year. Sweatshirt mornings that chill my breath into puffs of fog as I let dogs in and out from the deck are as welcome to me as the warm sunshine that follows.

Fall chores line up for us gardeners like so many K-Mart customers. Here are some we can't choose to forget.

1. Start a compost pile from the fallen leaves and debris from your garden. Don't add tomato or potato vines which are usually diseased. Continue to water any trees and shrubs you planted this past season. A thorough watering every two weeks up until the ground freezes will take them into the winter months in good shape. Cap any chimneys with wire mesh to prevent squirrels, raccoons, bats, and birds from entering or nesting in the early spring. Rake leaves off lawns to minimize snowmold damage. If you haven't time to rake your entire yard, make sure you rake and destroy leaves from beneath any apple or other fruit trees. If you have had any diseases in these fruits lately, chances are the leaves are carrying the disease, so get rid of them.

2. Protect young, thin-barked trees with tree wrap to prevent sunscald. Apples, maples and mountain ash are examples of trees commonly growing in our area that have thin bark. We can purchase tree wrap at local garden centers or hardware stores, but we can also use materials commonly found around the home. The idea is to shelter the trunk from sunlight and reflected light off snow during bright, cold days. Use a light-colored material that will reflect sunlight. Dark colors will absorb the heat from the sun and cause the bark to heat up. We can wrap these tender trees any time this fall before the snow flies. After springtime frosts vanish, these wraps should be taken off.

3. If you plan to feed birds this winter, it's a good idea to place feeders some distance away from buildings. Birds are notoriously sloppy eaters! Birdseed flies off in all directions and much of it ends up on the ground. This feed attracts other hungry animals which may decide to set up housekeeping in the nearest buildings. Gray and red squirrels are the most common critters, but the list could lengthen to include many other of our forest friends. A family of black squirrels are our nearest neighbors in our woods. I'll be watching for them at the new feeder we just put out. Be sure to store bird food securely in plastic or metal tins with heavy-duty lids to keep out mice and other rodents.

4. Autumn is our only chance to stock up on northern-grown apples. If you're lucky, you have Haralsons or Haralreds growing in your own back yard. Or maybe your neighbor has a tree that's loaded with apples and is willing to share them with you. One day this week I'm meeting up with my mom who has a huge box of Haralsons for me. She picked apples at a friend's house and is hoping I'll take some off her hands so she doesn't feel pressured into making a zillion pies for the freezer. I'm tickled! There's nothing better than an apple pie made from Haralson apples. Remember to treat apples like eggs. Handle them gently. Any bruises and they won't keep well. Store them in a cool, humid area and they'll keep until Christmas. Don't let them freeze.

5. Clean up the garden. Mow tall grasses and weeds that border the garden area. Insects and diseases are out there looking for places to spend the winter (they're not interested in Tucson or Orlando) and

garden debris and weeds always welcome freeloaders. Add a layer of composted manure and till or spade it under. Do all you can to get your garden in line for next spring. That way you'll be ready and in the starting gate as soon as the weather warms.

6. Clean and oil all your garden tools before putting them away for the winter. I'm always weak on this one. In fact, most of the time I forget where I put them from one season to the next. When we get a storage shed built just north of the house I'll feel more like getting garden tools organized. Right now they're in a cluster by the garage door. Check wooden handles on your tools and sand down and oil any that aren't smooth. There's nothing that takes the fun out of gardening faster than a nasty splinter in the thumb.

7. Continue to check pumpkins, squash, potatoes, carrots and any other harvested vegetables and fruits that are in storage. Remove any that show signs of spoiling. You remember the old saying about the one rotten apple ruining the whole barrel? It's true. Watch for soft spots on squash and pumpkins. If you catch them early, they will still be edible.

8. Plant amaryllis bulbs for giant holiday blooms. Buy paperwhite bulbs and nestle them in a container of pebbles or small rocks with water sometime in January. They'll reward you with fragrant flowers at a time when snowdrifts are high and winter seems cold and dreary. Plant a dozen bright tulips in a clump where you can see them from your kitchen window next spring. Cheery tulips do wonders for lifting our spirits and awakening our gardening souls.

9. Keep on mowing until the grass stops growing. Whew! We're tired of this job by now! Don't bother to catch clippings unless the grass is too long and the clipping are huge clumps scattered all over your yard.

10. Mulch your favorite rose, new bulb plantings and any other perennial you dearly love with straw, pine needles, or chopped leaves. Wait until the ground has frozen before laying on the mulch. I wonder how many times I have forgotten to mulch until the snow flies. So then I mulch on top of the snow and anchor it with some long pine branches.

11. This is a good time to plant a shrub unless we're knee-deep in snow. Shrubs adjust well to their new homes during the cooler temperatures of fall. The most important thing to remember is to make sure they go into winter well-watered. Frost and the cold reach down to the roots much easier if there are air pockets around the shrub roots. If these pockets are full of moisture, the frost/cold won't do much damage. Do NOT fertilize shrubs when they are planted in the fall. Fertilizer encourages spurts of new growth which won't have time to harden off before winter descends. Wait until early spring to fertilize.

CLEAN UP BEFORE HUNKERING DOWN

Our gardening chores aren't over. In fact, some of the most important work lies ahead. What we do this fall can save us a lot of time, effort and money next growing season. If we practice good soil management and gardening routines, we can cut down on the use of pesticides later on. The improvements we make to our gardening soils can make a huge difference when it comes to healthy plants next year. Healthy plants are less likely to succumb to diseases and pesky bugs.

First of all, we need to clean out our gardens of all plant materials and put them in our compost piles. This means getting rid of weeds, too. Many pests and diseases find a cozy place to hibernate in the dead leaves and stalks, and are ready to attack when spring comes again. A clean garden will eliminate such resting sites. It's a good idea to cut down tall grasses and weeds alongside our gardens for the same reason.

A walk alongside our flower gardens will remind us to tend to our perennials. These need to be cut back so there aren't a lot of dead leaves and stems to attract bugs. Later this fall we'll mulch over these perennials to keep them snug while cold winds blow. Clean straw and pine needles are good mulches because they are light-weight and yet insulate quite well. The other school of thought regarding protecting perennials is to leave all growth because it stops snow, thus making for deeper white mulch and less winterkill. Another reason to leave perennials is for their added winter interest. Some are downright lovely in the wintertime, peeking above the snowbanks with their seed pods and decorative leaves and flower heads. I do what I have time to do. But I ALWAYS cut back peonies to the soil line and get rid of the foliage which can be diseased. This helps control botrytis blight which can affect peony buds. Another perennial I cut back to 4 to 6 inches are irises, notorious disease-carriers. Once I get these two taken care of, I see what my schedule can handle.

The next step is to take down plant supports—cages, nets and chicken wire. Store these in an out-of-the-way spot. Now's also a good time to check over our gardening tools and see what we need to repair while the snow flies and we have extra time when we aren't out shoveling snow!

We can take all the dead plants we've just removed from our gardens and put them in our compost piles except for plants we know were diseased this summer. Watch out for tomatoes. Many of us may have had blight, so it's not a good idea to put this diseased plant material in with the healthy leftovers.

When our gardens are cleaned out it's time to till. A thorough tilling job this time of year will bring up critters that were sneaking down to find a winter hiding place. If you don't have a compost pile, another option is to remove all diseased material from your garden and just till the whole works in. This works with everything but corn cobs and stalks that won't decompose by the time spring comes. Remove these first.

Once all the leaves have fallen, we'll want to gather up all we can get our hands on and spread them over our gardens to a depth of 6 to 8 inches. Haul out the tiller and work these leaves into the soil. Then we can catch our breath for a couple of weeks and till the garden again if it hasn't frozen solid by then. Now we're in pretty good shape for planting next spring.

Keep in mind that adding dead leaves and other vegetation to our gardens doesn't necessarily improve its fertility. What it does do is condition the soil so it drains better and doesn't compact. It's really important that we do all we can to keep our soils well-conditioned. Seeds germinate better and plants have less trouble taking up nutrients in a healthy soil. If you question whether or not your soil needs to be fertilized or limed, take a soil test in the spring and send it down to the University (kits are available in the Extension Office). I always count on adding some fertilizer to my garden because nutrients leach out quickly in my sandy soil. Also, if we remember that our gardens contain many hungry plants in a relatively small space, it's no wonder that a garden needs to be replenished with nutrients every year. Corn, lettuce and broccoli, to mention a few, have huge appetites which drain a garden spot quickly.

Spend some time these chilly winter months browsing through seed catalogs. Look for seeds and plants that are hardy for our area and are resistant to diseases. We can do a lot to minimize disease problems by growing plants where THEY want to grow and NOT where WE want them to grow.

WASTE NOT—MULCH MUCH!

Before it gets cold, and I mean REALLY cold, we need to do some mulching. The best and most important kind of mulching material is the one Mother Nature sends down this time of year—the white fluffy stuff we shovel off our sidewalks, brush off our cars, and shake our fists at in March. Without good snow cover, many of our plants won't make it through the winter. Snow, comprised of moisture and lots of air, is the warmest, coziest mulch in spite of feeling cold to the touch. Beneath the snowbanks, roots of perennials, shrubs and trees are kept snug and warm. But Mother Nature, being a woman with a mind of her own, is unpredictable, which means we need to supply a considerable amount of our own protective mulch.

If it seems a bit late in the season for mulching, consider this. First, it's perfectly okay to add mulch on top of snow. Straw/leaves/pine needles on top of snow make an almost ideal haven for our plants slumbering underneath. They'll think they've gone to the tropics on holiday! Secondly, we need to wait for the ground to freeze well before adding mulch on top. If we add it too soon, the plants don't go into dormancy for the cold winter and will suffer winter die-back because they haven't become accustomed to any cold. Also, mulch added too soon before the ground freezes lures mice and voles into setting up housekeeping beneath the warmth. This means they'll be nibbling all winter long on the roots and bulbs that we're trying to protect. Be patient and let the ground harden first before finding your pitchfork.

Why mulch in the first place? Mulch stops the bitter cold from penetrating into the ground so easily and helps stop winterkill. But by far, the most value in mulching comes in the early spring when the snow begins to disappear and the sun starts to warm up the ground. The ground thaws when the sun shines and then freezes up again at night. A good, deep mulch will stop this process that is extremely hard on plants, since the sun can't reach the top of the dark soil with a mulch cover. Think about it. The sunshine that feels so warm as it pours through our windows in the spring can trick plants into thinking that winter is over and it's time to rise and shine. Even though we know in our hearts that spring rarely arrives in March, it's a tempting thought for both plants and people. Another plus for mulch is that it holds in moisture. Moisture keeps out the cold and frost, so again, mulch comes to the rescue.

What needs to be mulched? We'll go nuts if we have to mulch everything that we've planted! I try to keep this list quite short. First, I always mulch oriental lilies. They're borderline hardy in Zones 2 and 3, and since they're one of my favorite flowers, I want to keep them around as long as possible. Mulch any perennials/bulbs that are newly planted. If this is their first season, top them off with mulch for added security. If you've added any perennials that are listed as hardy for Zones 4 and 5, add them to your list. Russian sage comes to mind. My newly planted bed of irises is also on the top of my list. Irises are normally very hardy for our area. But as newly divided plants from my neighbor, they need some help this first cold season.

What are good mulching materials? Consider availability, cost and air-holding capacity. We have many red pine needles in our woods, and they make one of the best mulches around because they won't pack down. The air between the needles adds to their ability to hold in heat. They are easy to remove in the spring because they don't decompose quickly. They don't add acidity to the soil since they take several years to break down, and they are easy to find and move from the woods to my gardens.

Clean straw is an excellent mulch. It holds lots of air, doesn't pack down, is relatively easy to remove in the spring, and is usually available for a low price. A downside is that we have no idea how many weed seeds are being brought in with each bale. Old leaves, especially from oaks make good mulch. The veins in the oak leaves make them less susceptible to matting down and preventing air from getting in between them. On the downside, they are more likely to blow around than either pine needles or mounds of straw. Some gardeners use pine boughs if they are abundant. Never toss out the extra boughs from the bottom of your fresh Christmas tree. Put these on top of bulb beds to protect from the freeze/thaw cycle and from rodents and pesky rabbits whose tender paws don't like the feel of prickly needles. The boughs allow in some air and light so the bulbs aren't pressed down once they peek above the ground in early spring. Check mulched bulb beds often once spring rolls around and fluff up mulch when green bulb tips shoot up.

As for mulch removal, it all depends on the weather, and we know how unpredictable it can be. We don't want plants to suffocate; on the other hand, there's no sense in removing mulch too early so the freeze/thaw process gets the upper hand. Once night temperatures have warmed up so they are continually above freezing, it's usually safe to completely remove mulch. This is a task for gloved hands. A stiff rake can cause a lot of damage to tender spring shoots.

STEP THIS WAY
ON A PATH OF HANDMADE STONES

Stepping stones are so easy to make that even I can do it. Here's what we need for this project: 1 bag of Quikcrete (available at hardware and building supply stores for about $4.00), forms for the stones, 1 empty ice cream pail, a heavy-duty spoon, water, and items for decoration. It doesn't hurt to have a weight-lifter or wrestler around to tote the bag of cement. Weighing in at about 60 pounds, the bags are a real load! Keep in mind that one bag of concrete makes at least 4 stones.

Selecting the forms for our stones takes some thought. Functional stepping stones must be at least 1 1/2 inches thick in order to support our weight. If they're for decoration only, then they can be thinner. Stepping stone forms are available if you do some shopping. I saw some at our local Ben Franklin the other day. If you want to get fancy you may have to order from a special gardening catalogue. I settled on three of the clear plastic dishes used to collect drainage from flower pots. They cost around $1.00 at garden centers and are large enough to accommodate my size 8's! Almost anything can be used as a form, but remember that the thicker the form, the longer the stone will take to dry. Forms with straight sides are, in my opinion, more attractive than forms with angled sides such as pie tins.

An empty ice cream pail filled to within two inches from the top with concrete mix will make enough for about one average-sized stone. I plan to mix only one at a time because this mixture, once water is added, gets mighty cumbersome to handle. In fact, it's downright heavy! Choose a heavy-weight spoon for stirring. Anything else will bend in the process. Dump concrete mix into the pail and carefully add water. Stir in enough water so the mix is like heavy muffin batter. Relax—there's no way we can goof this up! If we add too much water, it will just take longer for the stone to dry. Dump the mixture into the form you've chosen. There's no need to line the form with anything, not even a spray of oil. The stone will drop out once it is almost dry.

Drag a straight board across the top of the stone to flatten it out. Put excess back into the pail. Let the stone sit undisturbed for about 30 minutes. Now it's time for the most fun of all, adding decorations. Here's where our creativity enters in. We can decorate with almost anything that comes to mind that is weather-proof —colorful marbles, shards of glass or pottery, ceramic tiles, you name it. Imprints are great ideas, too. Maybe you'd like your grandchild's hand or footprint in stone. I know a Master Gardener Grandma who has a path of stones decorated with imprints of her grandchildren's hands. She treasures them above all! Plant and tree leaves make lovely impressions in cement. Choose leaves with heavy veins so the imprints will show up well. Make sure to remove the leaves before the stone sets completely.

Now all we do is wait. Several days, in fact, depending on the humidity and the amount of water we added. Stones drying out indoors likely will be ready earlier than those left in the garage. We can tell the readiness by the color. The lighter grey the stone, the drier it is. Once several days have passed, tip the form over and carefully let the stone out. It's a good idea to do this close to the ground so it doesn't fall and crack unexpectedly. That's all there's to it. Gardeners turned artists—it's almost a miracle!

Winter ❧

Winter ❧

With one ear tuned to the radio, my sister and I quickly dressed for school in front of the fuel oil heater in the living room. It was the warmest spot in the house, especially with the northwest wind churning snow in every direction outside. With luck, we'd hear that school was canceled and there would be a "snow day." Most of the students at our school were farm kids, riding the school bus for miles before being deposited at the school's front door. This meant that everyone respected snowfalls, even the gentle ones that in a flash could become dangerous storms out on the prairie where I grew up. Blizzards still affect me the same way. Even though it has been years since I have set foot in a classroom, the anticipation of an unexpected day off gives me a boost of energy and has me adjusting the radio dial for the best weather report.

Blizzards are not the only reason I look forward to winter. The long, cold winter is a time for hibernating, for relaxing and reading the books and magazines that have been stacking up throughout the busy summer. Winter gives me time to take stock of the past growing season and my life's journey in general. I like the silence that comes from having windows tightly closed against the chilling winds. Often on the farm as I snuggled in bed on a really cold night, it was so still that I could hear the humming of the electric wires that connected to the house a few yards from our bedroom window. With only my nose sticking out from under the heavy quilts, I'd dream about beating my sister at checkers and Yahtzee, or maybe Monopoly or cribbage—games we'd play in the quiet winter evenings after supper dishes were done. And then, hearing the wind howl around the corners of the house, we'd pray for a snowstorm with drifts several feet high that would sequester us at home for a day or two more.

The thrill of the season's first snowfall still makes me reach for the phone to share the weather news with a friend. This is the sign we've been waiting for, the signal that winter, this naturally imposed separation between harvesting and planting, is upon us. Now the chronic humdrum of chores that could become tedious if left rolling on without a pause has come to a halt. With its solitude and peace, winter makes us sort things out and live with ourselves. And the result is that winter will give us a chance to start anew in the spring, to forget the past and begin again. No wonder winter appeals to me. There's nothing like a fresh start.

THE QUEST FOR A FRESH CHRISTMAS TREE

Fake, artificial, permanent—call them what you like, but you won't find one of these trees claiming center stage in our living room at Christmas! In fact, nothing in our house means Christmas more than a freshly cut tree. Growing up on the edge of the prairie meant that all of our trees were brought in from the hinterlands. They were so tightly bundled from the long trip that it took several days for ours to finally let down its branches and look like a real tree and not something from outer space. Shortly after my husband and I were married, we decided to give an artificial tree a chance. We thought it was quite lovely—fuller than many, and surely uniform and without holes or surprises. It was also without fragrance, character or charm. Since returning to the North Country, rich in real, live evergreens, that fake one has been sealed in the huge brown box it came in and deposited in a far corner of the basement. A real, fresh tree is our choice now, whether it comes from our own back woods or a neighborhood tree farm.

Choosing the perfect fresh tree for our homes can be a topic for lively discussion around the kitchen table. One wants a tall tree with short needles. Another dreams of a long-needled tree that's sprayed with artificial snow. Then someone has the bright idea of decorating the tree out on the deck for the birds rather than bringing it indoors. Most of these friendly chats discontinue once we arrive at the tree farm or woods where we can actually see what's available on the spot. Serious arguing starts at that point! The main consideration to keep in mind is whether or not the tree will fit in the spot we have ready for it. Amazingly, most trees have a way of looking so much smaller outside when surrounded by snow drifts, blue sky and other trees. Beware of this pitfall and always take a measuring tape along. Then be sure to use it!

Our tree this year fulfills my childhood dream of having a Christmas tree that reaches for the stars! Having cathedral ceilings in our home allows for a 15-foot tree that's almost impossible to decorate, but you won't catch me complaining! As a child, my heart ached for a humongous tree like the one that commanded the front of our small country church. But our farmhouse was small with regular 8-foot-high ceilings, so of course a tall tree was out of the question. That didn't stop me from dreaming. I'll never forget the year our dad came home with a puny tree that barely reached 5 feet. We were crushed. The solution was in a sturdy wooden box from the basement that served as a base for our tree. It solved the dilemma, but you can bet that the next year we insisted Dad shop earlier for our tree from the grocery store parking lot!

Knowing the difference between evergreen trees is helpful when it comes to selecting one from the woods or parking lot. Yes, they're all green and pointed at the top, but other characteristics are important as well.

Let's start with the long-needled varieties. The most common are the pines: white pine, red pine (also called Norway pine) and Scotch pine. Pines can be distinguished from other evergreens by their needles which grow in bundles of two (Scotch), two (Norway) and five (white). The way pines grow and are pruned often means the branches are tightly packed together. This can make it difficult to hang large ornaments. Needles, especially those of the white pine that are soft and feathery, don't hold ornaments well. The Scotch pine is a popular tree although not native to our country. Its branches are firm and it holds onto its needles better than other pines. Remember that pines usually have much wider bases in comparison to their height. An eight-foot pine may reach a width of six to seven feet. Now that's a fat tree!

Spruce are the most shapely of all. They are THE Christmas tree most of us have in mind when we envision a lovely, graceful tree full of old-fashioned ornaments. They have stiff, sharp needles, up to one inch in length. Their strong branches are excellent when it comes to holding ornaments. Spruce have that historic, comfortable look that makes them favorites for country homes. Many types of spruce grow in this country, but we're most likely to find black, white and Norway spruce in the northern areas. Keep in mind that spruces usually drop needles faster than pines or firs. This is especially true if it has been a dry growing season. If you have room for a tall tree with a slim figure, choose a spruce. But be prepared for sore fingers when decorating time comes around!

Last of all are my favorites—the firs. The balsam fir, which grows wild in northern states, is common and often easy to find, but the popular Fraser fir is native to the Appalachians, which means it commands a top price. Growers have introduced it lately to their tree farms so we can hope to see more of them soon. Firs make wonderful Christmas trees for several reasons. Their branches are spaced far apart so we can hang oodles of decorations. The dark green needles are flat with a silvery underside that's pleasant to the touch. These needles stay on the tree for a long time, or at least for three weeks, which is the maximum recommended time to keep a fresh tree indoors. But without a doubt, what I enjoy the most is their fragrance, as firs are the most aromatic of all evergreens.

No matter which type of fresh tree you choose, remember these tips. Always make a fresh cut (one inch minimum) before putting it in the tree stand. Sap quickly forms a seal over the original cut, making it impossible for the tree to take up water. A fresh cut will allow the tree to stay moist and fresh—and safe. Never let the tree go dry for the same reason. Keep a close eye on the water level, especially if the stand has a small water-holding capacity. Keep your tree away from all heat sources including fireplaces, heat ducts from the furnace, and appliances that give off heat. The cooler we can keep our tree, the longer it will last. If we lower the thermostat at night, our tree will stay fresher and our fuel bill will be smaller. If you get too cold, just reach for an extra blanket or let Fido into bed! A warm dog is worth an electric blanket any day in my book!

DECK THE HALLS WITH POINSETTIAS AND HOLIDAY CACTI

The left-over Thanksgiving turkey is hardly cool before the florist shops and discount stores have stacked high their assortment of holiday plants for the Christmas season. Highest and brightest in the entire selection is the poinsettia, long known and loved as THE Christmas plant. There are many reasons for its huge success. First and foremost, it is red! Secondly, it is relatively easy to grow, and third on our list of priorities is cost. When compared to other potted house plants, the poinsettia is inexpensive. I've seen handsome poinsettias for sale at discount stores for a meager $1.99. What a deal!

The poinsettia is native to Mexico where it grows outdoors as a large shrub. For you history buffs, the poinsettia is named after the U.S. Ambassador to Mexico, J. R. Poinsett, who discovered the plant growing in Mexico in the 1820s and brought it back to the States. Realizing that this plant is native to the warm climate of Mexico gives us some idea of its likes and dislikes. First, the poinsettia is sensitive to cold and needs protection from any cool breezes. This includes the interiors of our cold cars in December. The other factor is sunshine. To last until late spring when we can set this plant outdoors, we'll need to furnish our poinsettia with plenty of light. A cold, sunless room will mean the end for our holiday plant. Plenty of light and a bit of warmth will bring success.

The true name for the poinsettia is *Euphorbia pulcherrima*. Back in the 1800s when it was first brought to our attention in the U.S., it became a holiday plant due to its brilliant red leaves. Since then, hybridizers have been busy at work developing other colors. After a browse through a local florist shop recently, I can attest to at least eight other enchanting colors including peach, pink, white, green, and variations of all with stripes, flecks and patches of contrasting colors. There's undoubtedly a poinsettia for everyone, regardless of decorating tastes. With magical holiday names such as "Jingle Bells," it's no wonder we can't resist buying several of these beauties!

Poinsettias thrive if we keep several points in mind. Give them at least four hours of direct sunlight a day. A south or west window is perfect. Don't be afraid of giving them too much light but keep them away from drafts. This means drafts from cold windows and hot-air furnace ducts. Pick a calm, less-than-bone-chilling day to bring them home from the florist. It helps to heat up our cars first and to insist on two coverings for the plants before leaving the shop for the drive home. If not protected from the cold, our gorgeous poinsettia will drop its leaves before the first Christmas carol is sung! Because poinsettias don't require above-average warmth in their environment, our winter-heated homes are perfect with nighttime temps in the 50s to low 60s and daytime highs in the 60s to low 70s. Allow the soil to dry slightly before watering well. Give the poinsettia good drainage, which usually means cutting a hole in the shiny decorative foil wrapped around the pot and letting the water drain into a saucer or plate beneath the plant. Always use room-temperature water when watering plants. A cold shower is NOT what the poinsettia has in mind. Once most of the leaves have fallen (usually in late winter/early spring), cut the plant back to 8 or 10 inches and repot it in good potting soil. Set it outdoors in June once all threat of frost has gone. Find a bright spot where it will get good drainage and give it plenty of room since it will get quite bushy.

Before frost in the fall, repot the poinsettia, which will now be a small shrub, and bring it back indoors. If you appreciate a challenge, try to get it to flower again. It takes perseverance but is well worth the effort. When days begin to shorten poinsettias will automatically start turning color. All we have to do to make them gorgeous is to encourage this by providing them with a minimum of 14 hours of total darkness each night starting in September. We have some options in how we accomplish this. One year I wheeled mine into a totally dark closet when it was time to make supper. It also works to cover them with a double layer of dark plastic garbage bags. There is little leeway. Even forgetting one night can screw up the entire process. Setting a timer is a good idea for us forgetful folks. By November the new leaves will be turning color. It's quite a spectacular sight! By the way, the colorful parts of a poinsettia are actually leaves. The bloom is the center group of yellowish nubbins.

Another plant in the limelight around the holidays is the Norfolk Island Pine, true name *Araucaria excelsa*. The two growing well in our home have reached heights of four and five feet and are almost ready to be decorated as Christmas trees! They grow at least 6 inches every year, sending out a new level of branches that are covered with soft 1/2 inch needles. These pines like a lot of light but do best if the light is indirect or filtered (except in the winter when the sun is low and not so hot). Don't over-water a pine. Barely moist soil is the best. They can tolerate a wide range of temperatures and do well in the cooler temps of most winter homes. Another plus for us gardeners: they require little in the way of transplanting. Move them only when they outgrow their pots, which is maybe every 3 to 4 years.

Our grouping of holiday plants isn't complete until we add a holiday cactus. These cacti, along with the Easter and Thanksgiving cacti, are native to jungles rather than deserts and their names denote their blossoming season. By far, the most common is the Christmas cactus (*Zygocactus truncatus*) with clawlike stem joints about 1 to 1 1/2 inches long and 3-inch hooded tubular pink, red, white or multicolored flowers. These individual joints form arching, pendulous branches from whose tips hang the satiny flowers. They are stunning when in bloom and can exist in our homes for many years. It's not uncommon for a plant to be passed from one generation to the next. Give your cactus bright but filtered light. In order to get your cactus to bloom, it needs a cool-down period with night temperatures in the 40s and 50s. I leave my plant out in the screened porch until it's time for a frost. This ensures flowers. Once buds are set, daytime temps in the 70s with nights in the 60s are ideal. Keep the potting medium evenly moist (remember, this plant comes from the jungle). Fertilize every two weeks during the growing season. While the plant is resting (following the blooming period), keep the mixture on the dry side and don't fertilize. Christmas cacti propagate easily from stem cuttings by sticking a stem joint into peat moss or another light growing medium.

ABUNDANT EVERGREENS

How wonderful it is to live in the North Country where pines and other evergreens crowd in among the poplar and birch! It only takes a short stroll through the woods to bring back armloads of decorating materials from which to design a swag for the front door, a wintry welcome for the mailbox, and greens for the fireplace mantel. On the prairie where I grew up, evergreens were more scarce and, if there were any in the shelter surrounding our farmhouse, they were only the prickly spruce.

Growing wild in the woods protecting our house are red pines, soft-needled white pines, and balsam fir. I like to include branches from each in my decorations since they are so different from one another, not only in looks and texture, but in fragrance. Then, if I'm lucky to have any arborvitae growing by the garage after the hungry deer have meandered through, I'll add some of its flat leaves for an unusual color and aroma. Arborvitae, also known as cedar, must be as tasty to the deer as chocolate is to us!

Not everyone has a wooded acreage next door from which to select holiday greenery. If you're thinking of adding evergreens to your landscape, not only for decorating purposes indoors, of course, but also for outdoor beauty and shelter from northwest winds, there are several considerations. The first involves money. Evergreens cost more than deciduous trees. A small evergreen in a gallon-sized pot may cost as much as $30 depending on the variety. Another consideration is size. Evergreens, unless kept pruned, can become really large. The small arborvitae that's so neat and cute in the pot may grow several feet and end up covering your dining room window! Become knowledgeable about the mature heights and widths of the trees/shrubs you may want to add to your yard before you buy. Once they are purchased and in the ground, it's too late to take them back to the nursery.

Color and texture are other considerations. Green isn't just GREEN! Green can be yellow-green, blue-green and grey-green. Which ones will look good together, and which colors and textures will emphasize the size and color of your house? Are you interested in specimen plants (some evergreens become gigantic and we may have space for only one) or maybe a hedge to stop snow? Or perhaps we want foundations plantings that will look nice against our homes and coordinate with other shrubs and perennials.

To help out with our decision-making, it's a good idea to make a plan. First, make a diagramed plan of our house/acreage that's drawn more-or-less to scale. This doesn't have to be fancy. We need to include existing plants/trees/shrubs, sidewalks, anything we have that's permanently in place. We need to know the type of soil in our area. Is it heavy clay, loamy sand, or pure sand? What kind of sun/wind exposure do we get? These are all things to keep in mind when choosing evergreens.

Next, take a drive around your community/neighborhood. Which evergreens appear to be thriving? Ask your neighbors about their plantings. What success have they had with their choices? Most of us will have the best success with native plants, that is, trees and shrubs that grow naturally in the area. Exotics from other regions will likely struggle. Use other folks' experiences to help in your decision; that way you'll be less likely to make a mistake. If there are no balsam firs growing in your area, chances are there's a reason for their absence. Matching plants with their soil needs and horticultural zone is a step we must always consider.

As for my suggestions, here is a list of my favorite evergreens: balsam fir is generally not sold in garden centers because it's considered a "wild" tree and one that isn't propagated for resale. Balsam is also a bit dicey to transplant. This goes for moving one in from the woods, too. The smaller they are when transplanting, the better. Balsam is my favorite because it is so fragrant and its flat, green needles with grey/silver undersides hang on longer than needles from other evergreens. It prefers moist, cool soils with other trees planted nearby as a protective canopy.

I love having juniper nearby. A sprig of juniper adds fragrance and also a different texture to any holiday arrangement or decoration. There are many varieties that do well in the north country. Some are low-growing and creep along the ground while others reach 10 feet in height if left alone. Decide where you want it to grow before bringing one home in a pot.

Arborvitae or white cedar as it is sometimes called, has soft, green lacy foliage. It can grow in partial shade or dappled sunlight but can get winter burned if planted in full sun without protection from dry winter winds. There are many varieties of arborvitae, differing from each other in shape/size/hardiness. Some need more pruning/shearing than others. This is important when we consider the amount of time we have to spend gripping pruning shears.

Scotch pines have a somewhat twisted appearance and are picturesque with their orange-red bark. They are faster growing than others and make great Christmas trees. Spruce is attractive as a specimen tree, but keep in mind that it's slow-growing, takes up lots of space when mature, and has prickly needles. They are my least favorite when it comes to indoor decorations because, without a doubt, my bare feet will always find their dropped needles buried in the carpet until the Fourth of July. For sandy soils we can count on success with pines—Norway (red), Scotch, mugho—and junipers. Moist, heavier soils will support balsam firs and cedar, while Ponderosa pine do well in heavier clay.

Evergreens are usually grouped into one of these five categories: large and upright (recommended for specimen and accent plantings); upright and columnar (individual or foundation plantings); globular (accent in foundation plantings); medium-spreading (foundation plantings); and low-growing (ground covers). With this in mind, check out your area and see what your best choice will be. Remember to be patient. Evergreens are naturally slow-growing, especially at first. After several years of what seems like little growth, they'll usually shoot up quickly. In the meantime, when the holidays roll around and you want some branches for decorations, pay a visit to your friends who live out in the woods. Sounds like a good excuse for neighborliness and a cup of hot coffee!

AMARYLLIS REIGNS AS QUEEN OF WINTER FLOWERS

Like the Phoenix, the mythical bird of great beauty that rose from the ashes in ancient Arabia, the single amaryllis bud appears and ascends above the large potted bulb. One can almost see the stem inch its way up, reaching heights of 12 to 24 inches. This is the perfect flower for us kids of all ages to watch in open-mouthed amazement. Almost overnight it seems to add inches until it gradually opens trumpet-shaped flowers, two to four per bud, that measure 6 to 10 inches across. We gaze in absolute wonder as this gorgeous flower reveals its spectacular beauty.

Amaryllis bulbs show up all over this time of year, ready for gardeners to plant indoors. Considering their often inexpensive cost (around $5.00 for one bulb including plastic container and dirt), they make perfect gifts for gardening friends and holiday hostesses. Ever since I gave my mother one several years ago, she's been totally hooked and insists on getting several each December to give to neighbors and fellow church members. The bright reds seem to be favorites, although the popular Apple Blossom is a close second. Perhaps because the ground is white for many months during amaryllis season, the white-flowered bulbs aren't sought after and often are the ones left to be sold at discount prices. Other available colors are orange, pink, salmon and peach. Many have stripes and contrasting splashed markings. Regardless of the color, they are just the thing to brighten an otherwise blah winter day.

The true name for amaryllis is *Hippeastrum*, not that it truly matters! It is a tender bulb that won't survive northern winters outdoors, which makes it house-bound just like the rest of us. Amaryllis does best if given at least 4 hours of direct sun a day. Night temperatures in the 60s with daytime temps in the 70s are ideal. Our home is seldom an ideal growing environment for anything in the winter other than mites, but I find that amaryllis do just fine with temperatures even a bit lower than these recommendations. Amaryllis bulbs are large in comparison to most others available to us, and they like to live in close quarters. Plant them in a pot allowing no more than 1 to 1 1/2 inches on either side of the bulb. Most bulbs for sale this time of year come with a pot and soil included, but if you need to use your own soil mix, take equal parts of peat moss, packaged potting soil, and perlite or sharp sand. Cover the drainage hole in the pot with a few pieces of a broken clay pot or a fresh coffee filter so the potting mixture doesn't fall out. Fill the pot half way with soil, set the bulb in and finish adding soil. Be sure that at least 1/3 of the bulb is sticking above the soil. This may seem odd, but if the entire bulb is under the dirt the amaryllis won't do well. After firming the soil drench it well with water. Then don't water again until the bulb sprouts. Put the pot in the sun and begin regular watering, keeping the soil moist but not soggy. I also feed monthly with a water-soluble fertilizer as soon as sprouts appear. The new bulb doesn't need this extra food, but if I plan to keep the bulb year after year for blooms, it needs this fertilizer to keep flowering.

Once the stunning flowers appear, move the entire pot out of the direct sun. As with the rest of us, amaryllis flowers will fade and deteriorate if blasted with too much sun. When flowers fade (about two weeks later), cut the stem down to two inches and set the pot back in the bright sunlight. Don't you dare touch the leaves that have appeared! These strap-like leaves that can reach two feet in length must remain on the plant to provide food for next season. We must allow it to grow until the following fall when it will wither and die off. Now's the time to be sure to fertilize, at least on a monthly basis. Without fertilizer the bulb won't likely flower again. If you're lucky, another bud will pop up once the first one has finished blooming. It all depends on the health and size of the bulb. I usually set my amaryllis bulbs, pot and all, outdoors in a semi-shady spot once summer arrives. In the fall, before frost, I bring them back indoors, stop watering them, and set them in a dark, cool place in our house. This is the time for their nap. Some gardeners have good luck keeping amaryllis green and flowering all year long, but I prefer to give them a dormant time. After about three months I take them up from the basement, repot them in fresh soil (often keeping them in the same pot), and start watering again. Every three to four years they may need to be repotted into a larger pot, depending on whether or not new bulblets have formed around the base of the original bulb.

FORCING HARDY BULBS

Judging by the title, you may think this is a violent article leading to actions not permitted in a healthy community! Forcing ANYTHING has to be illegal! Maybe this horticultural term needs to be changed to "stimulating" or "coaxing" bulbs, since in actuality that's what we gardeners do to get them to bloom indoors. By artificially providing hardy bulbs with the 3 stages they need to go through in order to bloom, we can have tulips, daffodils and hyacinths in bloom during the middle of winter. Think of it! The beauty of spring without having to wait for it.

No matter where they're planted, indoors or out, bulbs must go through these three stages before they bloom: dormancy, deep root development, and sprouting. Dormancy, a time during which no active growth goes on, is brought on by summer's drought or winter's cold. For the hardy bulbs we have success with around here, this period is in the fall. Then the bulbs need to go through the second stage, a cool down, when they develop roots. They need at least 3 months of this cooling period. We call it winter. Don't we wish it were only 3 month's worth! For us to get hardy bulbs to bloom indoors, say in time for Valentine's Day, we need to provide them with this cold storage period where they won't freeze but just get mighty cold. An old refrigerator is perfect for this. A protected spot in your garage may also work. So will a root cellar that keeps things at about 35 to 45 degrees.

First of all, buy some new bulbs. Look for healthy bulbs with no soft spots or bruises. Low-growing varieties work the best since they don't need to be staked. It's your choice. Crocus work well. I also highly recommend hyacinths for their fabulous fragrance. They work better than any can of Glade to freshen up a wintry stale room. The miniature irises are lovely and so are the teeny daffodils. Grape hyacinths are a wonderful blue and help us create a delightful spring combination of blues/yellows/pinks with the addition of daffodils and hyacinths or tulips. One thing to keep in mind is the time for cool-down. It varies depending on the type of bulbs. Tulips usually need the longest time—12 to 16 weeks. Daffodils require 10 to12 weeks as do grape hyacinths and small irises. Hyacinths and crocus need less, 8 to10 weeks. These varying times become important when we decide to plant more than one type of bulb in a single container. Combined plantings can be especially attractive, but we need to plant those with like requirements together.

Select a planting pot with a drainage hole. Terra cotta, ceramic or plastic are equally good. Just make sure it's large enough to plant the bulbs you want so they're close together but not touching. I prefer wide, somewhat shallow pots that provide room for lots of bulbs and yet offer stability for plants that might otherwise topple over in a tall, narrow container. Scrub out the pot well, cover the drainage hole with rocks, pebbles or a coffee filter, and fill it 2/3 full with a growing mixture. A reliably good commercial potting soil will work. Ideally it will be about 1/3 loam, 1/3 humus or peat, and 1/3 vermiculite or perlite. Since I plan to replant my bulbs later in my garden (I can't bear to throw anything out!), I'm adding a level teaspoon of 10-10-10 dry fertilizer per quart of soil. This extra fertilizer will ensure that the bulbs won't deplete themselves of nutrition and energy. Moisten the soil with water, but don't saturate it.

When you pot your bulbs, plant them close together but not touching for a full, lush effect when they flower. Press the soil loosely around the bulbs. Sprinkle potting mix over them, adding soil until each bulb is no more than half an inch below the surface. Label each container with the date and variety of the bulbs it holds.

Now for the chilling phase. Potted bulbs must be kept moist and in a cool, dark place. Ideally, for the first 6 weeks, temps should be between 40 to 55 degrees. After that, during bud formation they can be even colder, down to 32 degrees, but not freezing. Check pots weekly to be sure they don't go dry. Too much dampness will rot the bulbs so take care not to over-water. I loosely cover my pots with clear plastic, which helps keep them from drying out.

Once our bulbs have completed their cooling phase, they're ready to be stimulated (forced!) into bloom. By this time we should be able to see roots coming out the drainage holes and pale yellow shoots peeking through the soil surface. We will introduce them to light and warmth gradually. This takes around 2 to 4 weeks. We don't want to rush this period by placing them directly in bright sun. The slower and cooler we bring bulbs along, the better quality our plants will be. Place pots in indirect light in temperatures around 55 to 60 degrees. Once they begin to bud out we can bring them into bright sunlight. They'll also need more light to keep them from getting too leggy. Rotate pots regularly or the shoots will lean off in one direction. Rather than forcing all of our pots into bloom at once (provided we've planted several), stretch the indoor blooming season by bringing out only one or two pots from cold storage each week. Snip off dead blooms once they're done flowering, and when spring arrives we can plant them outdoors in our gardens. It doesn't get much easier than this! Forcing—oops, stimulating—bulbs is a great project for kids of all ages. And remember, nothing beats fresh flowers indoors when there's a blizzard howling outside.

ARMCHAIR GARDENING

Armchair gardening is a terrific winter sport. When the northwest wind howls and the snow flurries fly, there's nothing better than to snuggle up in a cozy chair with a stack of garden catalogs and a cup of steaming hot chocolate. A warm furry dog nearby isn't all bad, either.

While the main fare of these catalogs seems to be flower and vegetable seeds, upon closer inspection we'll find other gardening supplies to fill our needs: tools, books and live nursery plants. Every living plant may begin as a seed, but let's face it, sometimes we need to hurry the entire process and just buy plants instead. This is certainly the case with trees, shrubs and some perennials. We do, after all, want to live long enough to see these plants grow and thrive. I know of some orchids that take several years to even germinate! Life's too short, I say! Bring on the live nursery plants!

Whenever possible I buy plants from local nurseries and garden centers. First, I like to see what I'm getting before paying out my cold cash. Buying in person means I can check the plant over and choose the healthiest specimen. Second, local growers know what plants are hardy for our area. Mail-order nurseries, on the other hand, may list plants that are borderline hardy. Locals know if the plant needs sun, shade, sand or clay. Plants will already be growing in containers and will be larger and better established than the dormant plants sent through the mail. Third, local nurseries need our financial support because they are paying taxes for our schools, police department and so on. While mail-order may sometimes seem less expensive, remember to tack on the shipping charges before reaching that conclusion. There are times, though, when ordering from mail-order nurseries is justifiable. They are likely to offer a wider choice of plant varieties than most local operations are able to do. For that truly special plant, we may find that we need to order it from a catalog.

If you decide to order live nursery stock, order from a reliable company. How can we tell one from another? I ask other gardeners. If they have had good luck from a company, chances are I will too. Beware of dealers that advertise miracle plants that grow a foot a day, repel mosquitoes, produce semi-loads of fruit from a single stem, and even do the supper dishes. Remember the old adage: "If it sounds too good to be true, it probably is."

Don't get lost in all of the gorgeous catalog photos. What we see isn't necessarily what we'll get! Professional photographers are hired to capture plants at their height of productivity under ideal conditions. I've never experienced this kind of Utopia, so always read the description of the plant first and then decide if it's for you. Colorful garden photos are entertaining but not always realistic.

Before we fill in the order form, we need to consider: Is the plant hardy for our area? Most companies list the hardiness zone in big letters. What is the average bloom time? If we're trying to keep our gardens blooming through the growing season, this is good information. Does the plant need sun or shade? What are the soil needs, sand or clay? How will it be shipped? What is the mature size? How about color? Once this information is clear, we can begin filling in the blanks.

Nowhere is timing more critical than in ordering live plants. Mail-order nurseries generally ship orders to arrive at the proper planting time, but it's a good idea to specify a delivery date. This is a tough call, considering the unreliable arrival of spring. As a rule of thumb, shrubs and trees can be planted as soon as the ground thaws. In the North Country, April is a good guess. Perennials usually respond to soil that has warmed a bit. The month of May is a good planting time. Most reliable companies will honor our requests as closely as possible.

If we prepare the planting site in advance we'll be a step ahead once our plants arrive. Choose a well-drained site, remove all grass and weeds, dig up the soil and mix in organic matter (unless we're planting beneath trees). Look plants over well when they arrive. If you see any evidence of disease or damage, contact the company right away.

Put healthy plants in the ground immediately. Soak the roots of bare-root trees, shrubs and rose bushes in a bucket of water for several hours before planting. Prune off any badly damaged roots because smooth wounds will heal faster than broken edges of damaged roots. It isn't necessary to soak perennials, strawberries, asparagus or potted plants unless the company directs us to do so. Always make sure that the hole you've dug is large enough so the roots are not crowded or bent. Wider is better, deeper is not! If nasty weather or a busy schedule keep you from planting right away, store dormant plants in a cool place, away from sun and winds. Perennial flowers may be stored in a perforated plastic bag in the crisper drawer of our refrigerators. Don't let them freeze. Don't cut them up for dinner salad, either.

Above all, remember that nursery stock is in a dormant state. They're napping. It can take anywhere from four to six weeks after being in the ground for them to come to life. Be patient. Keep them well-watered (a good soaking once a week) and mark them so you don't accidentally step on them or dig them up in order to plant something else.

CRITTERS ATTACK HOUSEPLANTS

Winter in the North Country isn't all bad. In fact, I appreciate the chance to relax and rest from mowing, pruning, weeding and planting chores. It also gives me time to check up on house plants that otherwise end up on the neglected side.

Houseplants need the maximum light available from our windows during winter. Plants that would burn up when placed in southern summer light can now be sitting on the window ledge. This is due to the low angle of the sun during these cold months. Putting plants closer to the window will help them survive this quiet season. Often this means we'll need to draw the drapes in the evenings so they don't catch a chill. Having clean, shiny windows is an added step in the right direction. Every time we water, it's a good idea to locate a magnifying glass to check for bugs. Winter may be the time our plants rest, but critters certainly don't.

Spider mites, a common bug found on ivy, flourish in the warm, dry conditions of our winter homes. Here's how to tell if you have a spider mite invasion. Hold a sheet of plain white paper beneath the leaves of the suspected plant. Gently tap the leaves several times; then inspect the paper. If you see what looks at first like dust particles moving around on the paper, you've got spider mites. They're about impossible to see with the naked eye. If left unchecked, spider mites can do a lot of damage. While it isn't a piece of cake getting rid of them, at least we can slow down their activity and, if we persevere, we can usually get them under control. A weekly shower either in the kitchen sink or the bathtub will deter them and often get rid of them if there aren't too many at work. A hand-held shower head comes in handy for getting a spray of water beneath the leaves where most smart bugs hide. If a few showers don't do the trick, we may need to use an insecticidal soap solution which contains a miticide, or another insecticide that's labeled for mites. Spider mites are members of the mite family and aren't a spider as the name at first implies. The reason they're called "spider" mites is because of the webs they often leave around plants when they are present in large numbers. While we can't see the mites, we often will see this webbing, an unwelcome sign indeed! Always follow directions when using an insecticide. Isolate affected plants if possible or their buggy visitors will hop on to the neighboring plant.

The mealybug often makes its presence known in the winter. You'll know that this critter has set up residence when you see fluffy white puffs on the branches/stems of a plant. These puffs aren't moving and are usually at the sites where the leaf joins the stem. This puff is a protection for the bug beneath that is busily sucking out plant juices. Look for mealybugs on succulents. I once had such a severe infestation of them on a jade plant that I had to get rid of the plant. I was heartsick. One non-toxic way to deal with mealybugs is to apply rubbing alcohol to each puff with an ear-swab. These are difficult bugs to kill off because of this white protective coating. Insecticidal soap is listed as a spray for mealybugs, and a repeat spray a few days after the initial one is recommended.

Aphids are everywhere. There are over 4000 species of them and most plants are susceptible to at least one. They are pear-shaped and less than 1/5 if an inch long. Their color varies from green to yellow to brown/black to grey. Aphids suck plant sap, leaving yellow and wilted leaves and deformed flowers. They secrete a sticky substance called honeydew that serves as a growing medium for an ugly black fungus called sooty mold. For outdoor plants, a jet of water from the spray hose is often enough to knock them off. This is a bit tricky indoors! Insecticidal soap sprays come to the rescue again. Aphids are visible to the eye and are so common that it's almost sinful. They don't fly nor are they particularly fast-moving, so a spray is usually effective.

Scale, a piercing-sucking insect that protects itself with its own armor can be an awful nuisance and is terribly difficult to control once it's in the plant's domain. Because of their dull color and limited mobility, scales often go unnoticed until damage has really been done. Look for them on stems and on the undersides of leaves along the major veins. Leaves of infested plants turn yellow and drop, and the entire plant loses vigor. Insecticidal soap is listed as a killer of scale. Horticultural oils can be used, especially on outdoor plants, which aren't our concern right now. A solution of rubbing alcohol and water brushed on with a swab or soft toothbrush will also control these critters. There are many kinds of scale insects but the one most likely to give us headaches is called the hemispherical scale. The shell of the mature female is a nearly perfect hemisphere, shiny and brown. Look for her!

The last critter worthy of mention is the whitefly. These are easy to spot once the infestation has grown. When we touch an infected plant, a cloud of whiteflies rises up and flits through the air. They quickly settle down and continue their dirty work. Rinsing plants weekly will help limit the numbers. Be sure to wipe off larvae and eggs from the undersides of leaves where they hide. Their preferred hosts include any citrus plants and poinsettias. They quickly move to neighboring plants and can be destructive if we let them get the upper hand. Insecticidal soaps and horticultural oils are recommended. I highly suggest weekly showers—that's for the plants. For us gardeners, make that daily!

Houseplants don't need fertilizer until they start to put on new growth in the early spring. Avoid watering houseplants every time you pass by them. Instead just whisper "hello." We kill off more houseplants by over-watering than anything else. Don't be afraid to get your testing finger dirty. Stick it into the pot of dirt and test for dryness. Most houseplants except ivies and ferns thrive if we let them dry out just a bit before watering them again. Then give them a long drink until water runs out of the drainage holes. This makes watering over a sink helpful. Cold water is out. Lukewarm water is best, every season of the year. Forced air furnaces save us from freezing to death, but they blow dirt and dust around for months that accumulates on furniture and plants. A monthly lukewarm shower to remove dust buildup helps plants photosynthesize. Remember, they're struggling already with the low availability of light this time of year. Help them out by keeping them free of dust and pet hair.

Sidewalks get treacherous during the winter. We can shovel all we want—or don't want which is my category—but often there still exists a layer of ice. Instead of reaching for the salt bag (sodium chloride), try getting by with sand or chicken grit, which I like even better. It's sharp and improves traction a lot. Some folks think wood ashes do the trick, but unless you don't mind having them tracked all over the house, I'd advise against them. The reason wood ashes may seem helpful in slick areas is that they are dark and absorb the sun's rays which in turn help melt down the ice. Most of the ice around our house is on the north side, which never catches a ray of sunlight. Salt works the best to dissolve ice, but it isn't good for surrounding shrubs and plants. Information on the salt bag might claim that it's safe around plants, but I still think it's a better idea to use sand or grit. I always pack a bag of grit in the trunk of my car in case I get stuck in a snowbank somewhere.

Prune large shade trees in the mid-to late winter. Even maples that will bleed (of course this is just sap and not real blood!!) can be trimmed this time of year. For really tall trees it's best to hire a professional. We amateurs who don't know what we're doing can get in big trouble if a tree or large branch falls on a power line or onto our neighbor's fence. Most of the time the main pruning that needs to be done is cutting back any branches that are rubbing on our house or other building, or branches that are getting too close to power lines. Be careful.

Snow and ice on evergreens may cause some damage, but we could make matters worse by trying to remove it. Trees are brittle in the cold. If we come along with a broom and give them a whack to remove snow, we could easily snap off branches and injure the tree/shrub. If you feel you must remove some of the heavy snow, use your broom to lift from beneath the branch and gently shake it off.. There's less likelihood of damage with this approach. Otherwise, let Mother Nature take her course and wait until the weather warms.

OUTDOOR WINTER INTEREST & INDOORS WITH
PAPERWHITES AND HYACINTHS

"Any flower in winter" is equal to "Any port in a storm" in my book! The whiff of a delicately scented flower and the glimpse of unfolding petals is enough to sustain us gardeners while the landscape is white and bleak. Enter bulbs to the rescue!

Of all the bulbs that will flower indoors, the easiest are the tender tazetta narcissus that we commonly call "paperwhites." They can be grown in pots with soil or just in water. If they are grown without soil the bulbs exhaust themselves and aren't worth saving after they bloom. But they're worth the money anyway. My only regret is that they aren't paperpinks or paperreds which would be much more welcome as we are surrounded in this white wonderland called winter. Paperwhites are quick growers and, if started in soil in September, will bloom well before Christmas. If you choose to start them in soil, put them in with their tips just below the soil. Paperwhites don't need to go through a cool-down cycle to produce flowers as do tulips, daffodils and other hardy bulbs. For this reason they are quick and easy. Use a regular potting soil and a pot with drainage.

If you're feeling a bit lazy like me and prefer to grow them in water, you'll need to have something in the water to anchor the bulbs. Aquarium sand works as do marbles, small stones, and any decorative glass pebbles. Crowd as many bulbs as possible in a decorative bowl. I like to use clear glass so the roots are visible. A tall, clear glass vase is the best choice since it will allow the light in to the bulbs while supporting the leaves and stems which tend to topple over. Be sure the bulbs themselves aren't resting in the water; only the base of the bulb should be touching the water line. As the bulbs begin to sprout, keep the roots covered in water. Move the pot to a bright window and rotate the pot as the bulbs send up foliage. This will usually take 2 to 3 weeks.

Once the paperwhites begin to flower, move them to bright but indirect light so the flowers last longer. If they begin to bend or lean toward the light, it may be necessary to stake or tie them up. Green bamboo sticks or natural-colored stakes blend in well as do green twist ties and green twine. For a decorative touch, use raffia ties or other ribbon. Be prepared to wear a clothespin on your nose if you get too close to blooming paperwhites! Some folks think they stink! I prefer to call them "fragrant," and during this season of cold and darkness, it's as welcome as wood smoke and pot roast.

For a heavenly scent and downright elegance, force a hyacinth bulb in water. A helpful device is the hourglass-shaped container designed especially for this purpose (I also use these containers for paperwhites). Hyacinths forced hydroponically, as this method is called, must be purchased already "prepared" and ready to grow. This means they have gone through the necessary cool down period prior to sale. Be sure to ask about this before purchasing bulbs since not all hyacinths are ready for this type of forcing. Fill the glass up to its narrow waist with water. Set the bulb in the upper section of the container so the water just reaches the base of the bulb. To promote root growth, it's helpful to set the bulb in the container in a dark corner. In about 2 to 3 weeks it will be ready to bring out into bright light. Maintain the water level so it just touches the underside of the bulb. As with paperwhites, this hyacinth bulb will be useless once it has been grown by this watery method, so don't plan to stick it in your garden next spring. Just delight in its color, beauty and fragrance during these gray, snowy days.

Now is the time to take stock of the outdoor shrubs and perennials surrounding our home and notice which ones look interesting during the winter. Most of the time when we plant outdoors we only think of the luscious tomatoes that we'll harvest in 74 days, or the aromatic lilies that we hope the deer won't chew off. Let's face it, our minds are far from winter when we're outdoors in June with our spades and trowels. But there are plants/shrubs that offer showy contrast from winter's snowbanks, and now's the time to appreciate them and consider new plantings for next season. I was delighted to see the flock of cedar waxwings descend upon our Red Splendor flowering crab. This flowering crab is an excellent choice for our northern area with its hardiness and showy apples that cling to the tree instead of falling to the ground or sidewalk. The waxwings made quick work of the fruit and now both fruit and birds have vanished. The hips from shrub roses are colorful as are the heads of Queen of the Meadow Filipendula that I don't cut back in the fall because I'd rather see it wave above the snow. Red-twigged dogwood stands out against the whiteness and is an excellent shrub for moist areas. Heads of purple coneflowers and decorative grasses contrast with the snow and also offer food for the birds. The next time you visit your gardening neighbor, take note of the shrubs and other plants that break up the monotony of pure white in their yard/garden. Which might you want to plant next year? Write them down before you forget.

WINTER BLOSSOMS TAKE AWAY WINTER BLAHS

Nothing brightens my sagging spirits quicker than a good mystery novel or a flowering plant, except, of course, for a trip to Hawaii! But let me assure you, a book and a plant are far more accessible due to our starving post-holiday bank account and the latest fill of fuel oil. The trouble with flowering plants is that they require more light than foliage plants. But don't let that discourage you from adding one to your winter decor. The need to surround ourselves with beauty exists even during the darkest winter days, and with a little extra tender loving care (TLC), we can keep a plant in good blooming shape until spring when it's time to start outdoor chores.

Tops on my list is the Cyclamen. They remind me of butterflies dancing along the top of my garden during the summertime. Cyclamen is a popular plant available at most garden centers and even in grocery stores this time of year. The spectacular blossom colors range in all shades of pink, red, coral, purple and white, which is undoubtedly the least popular in our snowy part of the world. Who wants a flower that reminds them of a snowdrift? We need color, not more white! What makes these flowers so unusual is that the blossom is carried high above the leaves, appearing to hover and nod about with the least amount of breeze. Keep a cyclamen in bright but indirect light. They need moist soil; don't let it dry out. On the other hand, the tuber will rot if it's soggy, so don't over-water either. Since they thrive in cooler temperatures (low 50s at night, mid-60s by day), they find our cool winter homes ideal. Not only are the blossoms lovely, but the leaves, most sporting silvery markings, are attractive as well. After the plant stops flowering, usually in late spring, it's time to repot it. Place the tuber in fresh potting soil so it's about half out of the soil mix. A good quality light-weight potting soil works best. If you mix your own, use 1 part potting soil to 1 part sharp sand and 2 parts peat moss. It's possible to start these lovely plants from seed, but it takes forever. I recommend buying a blooming plant now, in the mid-winter, when we need a colorful shot in the arm. Patience is in short supply these days.

There are few flowers lovelier than the hibiscus. I'd much prefer enjoying these beauties in their native surroundings—the warm Pacific Islands, for instance. But since that's not possible, purchasing one is the next best thing! The fragile papery beauty of the hibiscus enchants many a gardener and except for the pests they attract, aren't all that hard to grow. The challenge is keeping them warm enough in our cool houses. Being from the tropics (most of our house plants are, by the way) hibiscus love warm weather. They like at least 4 hours of direct sun daily with night temps in the 60s and days in the 70s or higher. This rules my house out! It also means they have to be a distance from windows. Hibiscus likes moist soil, frequent fertilization, and once it's in a preferred spot, dislikes being moved around. They can get to be tall plants so prune them back when you feel they're getting out of hand. In the spring, it's relatively easy to take stem cuttings of new growth. Hibiscus flowers, which seldom last more than a day, range from white through yellow, salmon, orange, pink and scarlet. Give this plant at least two wraps with paper/plastic before taking it home from the florist on a cold winter day. It helps to have the car warmed up, too.

Kalanchoe (pronounced kal-an-ko-e) is a winter flowering plant with masses of four-petaled flowers that may nearly cover the waxy thick leaves. Blossoms are long-lasting and are usually in reds or yellows. They need 4 hours of bright, direct light daily and do well in cooler temperatures of nights in the 50s, days in the 60s. Don't overwater these plants. Let them become nearly dry between thorough waterings. Kalanchoe requires less care and fuss than either the cyclamen or hibiscus. Given enough light, it will take care of itself and tolerate more neglect. Now we're talking!

With St. Patrick's Day coming up, we'll be seeing oxalis popping up in the stores. The shamrock-shaped leaves of this delightful plant make us think of it as a foliage plant, but it does flower and when it does, you'll be charmed. Oxalis is a bulb plant, growing about 6 to 8 inches high although some varieties may be a bit taller. The small flowers open on sunny days and close at night—just like our eyelids! In fact, I think the entire plant closes down when the sun sets. I know the feeling! The variety I have sports white flowers but I've seen other varieties that are pink. These plants like light and cool temperatures. They don't like to dry out, so keep the soil moist. Fertilize while plants are actively growing. Oxalis definitely goes through a dormant period when they need to rest. At this time we can let the soil dry out and replant the bulbs in new soil, or we can let the bulbs rest in the pot and begin watering/fertilizing when we see them show signs of growth, usually 3 months later.

Without question, African violets are the most popular flowering house plant. There are a gazillion varieties available with new hybrids constantly being developed. With proper care, these violets bloom almost continuously. They stay relatively small, anywhere from 4 to 8 inches tall, which makes them adaptable to most homes. The velvety clusters of flowers come in pinks, blues, purples, whites and all sorts of interesting bicolors. These 1 to 2-inch flowers may be smooth, ruffled, or frilled and are in the centers of the rosette-like hairy leaves. Give African violets lots of indirect light to keep them blooming. A neighbor grows them so successfully and, since she denies having a green thumb, the reason for success must be in the light they get from all the glass doors in her home. They aren't fond of cool temperatures, favoring instead nights in the high 60s to low 70s, and days up in the 70s and 80s. Water to keep the soil barely moist, being careful not to get water on the leaves. African violets like the humidity that comes from setting them on a tray of pebbles with moisture beneath. Take care so the bottom of the pot doesn't come in contact with the moisture beneath or the plant will suck up the moisture and become too wet.

Gloxinias remind me of gigantic African violets. The real name for this popular plant is *Sinningia speciosa*. They are a tuberous-rooted Brazilian wild flower with velvety bell-shaped blossoms that can be up to 6 inches across. They come in white, pink, deep red, lavender and purple, often edged or spotted with contrasting hues. These gorgeous flowers are held slightly above the compact growth of velvety, oval 5-inch leaves. They may blossom at almost any time and then go through periods of dormancy. Similar to the African violet, the gloxinia does best in bright indirect or curtain-filtered sunlight. Nights in the 60s with days in the high 70s are ideal. Keep soil moist (don't let this one dry out) and fertilize monthly when plants are growing. Stop fertilizing when flowers fade, and gradually reduce watering until foliage withers. Now is the time for a couple of months' snooze. When you notice new sprouts from the tuber, repot in a fresh mixture and begin water/fertilizer. As with violets, gloxinias like an acidic soil mixture. These are available commercially.

FLOWERS FOR YOUR SPECIAL VALENTINE

Valentine's Day often sneaks up on me. How, you may ask, can this happen during a season of snow flurries, white outs, leaf-less trees and icy sidewalks? It's easy. This is my catch-up season. Friends who were ready to look for my name in the obituary column are now hearing from me. New recipes are being tried in the under-used kitchen, books are being read that just collect dust during the summer, and drawers and shelves that suffer hang-overs are being tidied. Days are too short to get all accomplished that I have on my list. Valentine's Day is a welcome surprise, a cause for celebration between Christmas and Easter.

How do you remember your Valentine? I have a friend who claims that his wife will serve him with divorce papers unless she gets a box of chocolates! To him I advise getting her more chocolates! But to the rest I proclaim the virtues of non-caloric, highly satisfying plants and flowers. Every now and then my husband amazes me. Last year he came home with a bundle of my favorites, Stargazer lilies and blue irises. The irises didn't last as long as I had hoped, but the overall combination of blues and pinks was breathtaking! And of course we could smell the Stargazers even before we entered the great room area. What could be better? Well, maybe the smell of pizza baking in the oven at 6:00 p.m.

The most popular Valentine flower is the rose, and not just ANY old roses will do. They have to be red ones, the long stemmed variety. I took a peek into the refrigerated area of a local florist a year ago and was absolutely amazed at the number of roses they had on hand for the biggest sales day of the year—and most of the roses were red. Why? Because historically the red rose symbolizes love more than any other flower.

The life of a cut rose is short, but there are some things we can do to prolong its beauty. First, mix up the floral preservative that accompanied the flowers. Most florists send these packets along at no charge. This is NOT plant food, but rather a combination of ingredients that stop bacteria from growing and clogging up the pores of the plant stem. When this bacteria grows in the water, it stops the flower from taking up water which means it will wilt and die. Next, select a sparkling clean vase for the flower. One with a wider bottom than neck will make it more stable and less likely to tip over. Before arranging the rose stem, make a fresh cut while holding the stem under water. This will stop the plant from sucking up an air bubble which will get in the way of the water reaching the blossom. Quickly slip the rose into the container and set it in an area out of the direct sun. Keep it away from drafts including the forced air register from your furnace, and of course don't set it on top of the television or close to any other heat source. Cooler is better. There's a reason florists spend so much money on refrigerators for their flowers! If you have room in yours, stick your rose in there overnight and it will thank you.

Many gardeners love the bulb dish gardens. These are among my favorites as they bloom over a long period of time. Many of these bulb gardens contain a vareity of bulbs, crocus, miniature daffodils, hyacinths, and tulips being the most popular. I saw a lovely composition at a florists last week. The garden was arranged so the larger bulbs were at the rear of the container. Then a small nest with eggs was nestled in some moss up front. To tie it all together was a tangled loop of curly willow. The effect was spring-like and earthy. I wanted it right away! The advantage of these bulb gardens is that we can repot the bulbs in the fall in our own gardens. With this in mind, it's not a bad idea to take really good care of dish gardens. Don't let them dry out but don't get them soggy, either. Fertilize bulb gardens every other week with half-strength fertilizer, give them plenty of light and keep them cool.

Although roses may be the flower of choice for your special Valentine, they are pricey. There are other cut flowers that will last longer and not cost so much. If your sweetheart longs for a trip to the islands, opt instead for an exotic bouquet of birds-of-paradise. For fragrance, oriental lilies such as the Stargazers I mentioned earlier can't be beat. Mums are always available in a variety of colors and alstroemeria, also called Peruvian lily, will last for many days in an arrangement.

As for a potted plant, miniature roses are showing up all over in time for this lovers' holiday. While they are petite and lovely, don't count on being able to keep them alive until planting time. Quite likely they aren't hardy for our cold climate anyway. But that's not to say they aren't a good choice for Valentine's Day. They're a lot less expensive than long-stemmed roses, and are quite lovely while in bloom. Anthuriums always show up in florist shops in February. You'll recognize these right away with their heart-shaped, waxy flowers (usually red or pink) with the tail-like structures called spadices sticking out like a pebbled tongue. This tongue contains the true flowers of this unusual plant. The glossy bracts just draw our attention (and the attention of pollinators) to the flowers. The anthurium is a true native to the tropics. They do best in bright indirect light with nights in the 60s and days at least in the 70s. Keep them moist and fertilize every two weeks. If you really want a challenge, try your hand (and your wallet) at orchids. These require some extra learning on our parts as there are few that will thrive in our regular households, Many new hybrids are becoming available which means lower costs. They are truly unique, interesting plants and worth a try if we can buy them without paying an arm and a leg.

Creating a living wreath will keep our gardening fingers occupied and out of trouble until spring gets here. A living wreath is just that - a wreath made of living rather than dead plant materials. Living wreaths make attractive center pieces when lying flat. They can also be hung up on the wall if created with that in mind. Start with a circular form made of compressed peat. Garden centers often carry these in several sizes. To choose the best one for our purpose, we'll need to know where we eventually want to place it. The next step is to soak the form in water until it's saturated; this can take several hours. Once thoroughly moist, it's time to do the planting. This can get messy so choose a site accordingly. My kitchen counter is always the easiest spot to clean up. Being near the coffee pot and telephone make it near-perfect. Many types of plants look attractive in a living wreath, but my suggestion is to use slow growing ones which will eliminate a lot of pruning and training on our parts. I use succulents; jade works well as do varieties of sedum. You might want a wreath of just one plant. On the other hand, a wreath of various textures, shapes and colors is interesting. Let your creative juices flow. Using a small pointed instrument (the pick from our nut bowl is perfect!) make a small hole in the wreath for a cutting. Dip the end of the cutting in rooting compound (available at garden centers) and then into the hole. Press gently around the hole to seal in the plant. Continue inserting cuttings all around the wreath. When done, put the wreath in a plastic bag in which you've made several breathing holes; set it in a shady spot for several weeks until the cuttings have taken root. Keep an eye on the wreath to be sure the plants are getting enough air and yet not drying out. Wreaths can support plants for a long time if we give them additional nutrients at watering time. Watering isn't as difficult as it sounds. Set the entire wreath on a large cookie sheet and give it a good soaking. Drain off any excess water. Wreaths need an occasional trimming to keep them looking attractive. Use your judgement when you think this is necessary. Use the trimmings to make a wreath for your gardening neighbor.

PLAN BEFORE PLANTING

This year I'm going to have the BEST garden ever! I wonder how many times I've said that to myself long about the end of March when I'm itching to get started in my garden. A dash of optimism never hurts when you consider the obstacles that we gardeners have to face in North Country Zone s2 and 3!

First things first. I need a plan. Gardening can be compared in some ways to going on a summer journey in our car. We'll likely reach our destination either with or without a map, but a map will take out the guesswork and help us stay on the right highway without getting lost on the backroads. Likewise, a garden plan will organize our green thumbs and help us make room for whatever we want to plant without forgetting something important.

I will need to make several lists. The first will be of the seeds I have to buy this spring. Some seed packages that I kept overwinter in a tight jar in the refrigerator contain leftover seeds. These should germinate well since they were kept cool and dry, although I probably can't expect the germination rate of last year. I never have extra zinnia or marigold seeds, and more than likely the pea and bean packages are empty.

What transplants will I plan to buy this year? Should I start my own cabbage? Maybe I'd be better off buying the two packets of plants that will keep our family of two in enough coleslaw until the snow flies! I always like to start my own tomatoes, broccoli and peppers because I enjoy watching them grow, and somehow manage to find room for a lot of them in my garden. But if I need only a few plants of a particular crop, it's easier and cheaper to buy them as seedlings from the nursery. April is a good time in our area to start peppers and tomatoes. Broccoli, too, if we plan to set it out in mid-May. One common mistake we often make is in starting our seeds too early. Unless we have an artificial lighting arrangement for our small plants that gives them 12 to16 hours of light per day, we'll end up with spindly plants if we get too impatient with sowing our indoor seeds.

What did I plant last year that didn't work out as well as I had expected? What was so wonderful that I'll want to plant it again this year? Here's where some record-keeping comes in. I'm not talking fancy records. Almost any kind will do. Old seed packages rubber-banded together. Photographs taken of our gardens with notes jotted on the back. We have to know what we planted from year to year so we can make good choices for the next year It's hard to go somewhere unless we remember where we've been! I KNOW for certain that I'll include nicotiana in my flower bed again this year. It bloomed like crazy way up until frost. I'll also have another hill or two of Johnny's Passport Melon. Its sweet, green flesh was a real treat last summer. I didn't think much of the Sundrops squash or the crowds of black peppers. These peppers were fun for a change, but I missed the bright green ones for stuffing.

An actual garden layout on paper complete with guestimated distances will stop me from trying to cram too much into too small a space. If I put it down on paper first, I'll have time to organize it and leave room for air circulation and my small tiller. Last year I set my tomatoes right down the center of my garden. This year I'll move them over to one side. A bit of crop rotation can help cut down on diseases although it's not as effective in a small garden area as in a larger one.

Sometime soon I'll call up a local farmer and order a couple loads of well-aged manure for my sandy garden. A soil test which was sent to the University showed that my soil is neutral, but I know it's low on organic materials so every bit of compost helps retain moisture and hold nutrients. How about your garden size? Do you try to farm your entire back yard? OR do you keep it down to a size that's manageable for you so it doesn't seem overwhelming when weeding and harvesting? I can still hear my husband's voice: "It's YOUR job to grow the vegetables and MY job to eat them!" And eat them he does! But the planting, fertilizing, watering, thinning, weeding and picking is up to me, so I keep my garden small. When it becomes more work than fun, then I figure something's wrong somewhere.

The early blast of winter caught many of us by surprise last fall. The snowfall kept us from raking leaves and now we're faced with the mess this spring. As soon as the soil dries, the wind stops blowing and our backs feel strong, we can get out there and rake. Early removal of leaves and debris will stop molds from growing in our lawns.

Are you ready to forget winter by packing away your favorite woolen sweater? Be sure you launder or dry clean it first. Carpet beetles and clothes moths like to feed on fabric of animal origin, especially any items that are soiled. Then store that sweater in a tight container like a chest or box. Avoid plastic bags for long-term storage as there could be some moisture problems, or reactions between plastic and fabric. If you can stand the smell of mothballs, you can add them to the storage container as they give added protection from these critters. Cedar chips are not effective although they certainly smell good!

Keep an eye on your spring-flowering bulbs and rhubarb that may peek above ground soon. You may need to toss on some mulch if the temperatures dip way below freezing.

FRUIT TREES NEED PRUNING

Last fall, in a moment of weakness, I volunteered to help a friend prune her apple trees. She called yesterday to ask if I really meant what I had said, or if I was just fooling. Truth is, I had forgotten all about it! But I know she'll have a cup of coffee ready for me, and with the two of us armed with pruning shears, the task should be a quick one.

Early spring is the perfect time of year to prune fruit trees and trim out dying wood from shade trees in our yards. It's easy to see what we're doing since old leaves are dead on the ground and new ones haven't popped out yet to get in our way. Sappy trees such as maples and birch will flow heavily this time of year, so unless there's a lot of deadwood hanging dangerously from them, wait until fall to trim them back.

Wait for flowering shrubs to flower before trimming them. Lilacs are an example of early flowering shrubs that set buds in the fall. If we get too handy with our pruning shears in early spring, we'll nip those buds right off and end up without flowers this season.

Are we ready to prune? Not quite yet. Let's make sure the pruning shears are sharp. Dull blades leave jagged edges and can tear bark without making a clean cut. It's a good idea to tote along a pail of disinfectant solution (about 1/2 cup of household bleach per quart of water). We'll dip our pruning shears into this liquid between cuts as a precaution against spreading disease. This is especially important when pruning fruit trees that have been stricken with fireblight.

There's no need to paint cuts with any wound dressing. This sticky, gooey stuff is impossible to work with when temps are cool, and it really isn't necessary. Healthy trees will heal themselves quickly without this goop.

We prune fruit trees for two basic reasons: to encourage production of fruit, and to maintain the beauty of the tree. Common sense tells us that it's best to start training young fruit trees as soon as we plant them and before they get too tall and out of hand (it's a lot like raising kids and dogs!). If, as in the case of my friend's apple trees, a pruning shear has never been within ten feet of the tree in years, it's best to prune a little each year until the tree shapes up. If we prune too much at once, we'll encourage the growth of water sprouts. Then we'll just have to prune out these water sprouts next year. Water sprouts are easy to identify, especially when they're young. They grow quickly, several feet in one season, and sprawl wildly in every which direction. They remind me of the cowlick I get on top of my head when my hair is cut too short! So a little pruning here and there will do it this first season. An all-over haircut will cause more problems than we had before.

On older trees, we'll start out with corrective pruning. First we'll clip out any dead parts. Then we'll take out any crossing branches that rub against main limbs, and any that grow toward the center of the tree. One of our goals is to open up the tree so that sunlight can reach the branches. Sunshine does for trees what it does for us humans: boosts our energy and makes us bloom!

Apple and plum trees have small twigs called spurs that grow close to the branches. Blossoms form on these spurs, so we'll be careful not to prune these off. We'll take out some of the old wood that doesn't have many of these spurs. If my friend's trees are really tall, we might cut the tops back a foot or two. But we'll keep in mind that we want the tree to look better AFTER we pruned than before, so we won't give it a "butch" cut. If we cut the top back too much, we could ruin the looks of the tree. Use your eyeballs when pruning so you don't cut off more than what looks good. Then we might call it quits until next season. Old trees will need more than one year to recover and become productive again, so don't rush out to buy extra pie tins and canning jars yet.

If you have a young fruit tree, you'll need to do extra work. First, determine the leader which is the strongest point growing vertically from the trunk. Then prune back the other tips that are in competition for leadership. Small, bare-root fruit trees usually have only one main leader which makes this task easy. If a tree has several leaders, they will form narrow crotches where they join. These crotches will be weak and tend to break, especially when the tree is loaded with fruit. Once the leader is chosen, snip it back if it is too tall. A desired height of a newly planted tree is around 10 feet. After choosing one leader, select the first or lowest branch of your tree. It should be at least 2-3 feet from the ground which allows room for mowing underneath it. It's important that all of these scaffold branches, as they are called, have wide angles where they join the trunk. The first year of training usually produces a leader and two or four branches. New lateral branches will grow from the leader next year and from these you can choose another scaffold branch or two. Ideally the space between scaffold branches should be from 8 to 16 inches or so, with branches evenly distributed around the trunk. Don't be afraid to make cuts. If you have questions about initial pruning, ask the folks from the nursery where you purchase the tree to help out.

Keep these general points in mind when pruning fruit trees: Cut close to the trunk but leave the "collar". This is the swollen ring on the branch right next to the trunk. Don't leave stubs sticking out. Prune a little every year and start when the tree is young. Keep the center of the tree open so fruit will ripen. Never prune more than 1/3 of the tree in any given year/season.

My gardening friend, Cathy, offers this tip for all of us green thumbers who are starting seeds in flats: small wooden spoons make dandy labeling sticks. They're small enough to poke into our starting pots without causing trouble, and yet the spoons gives us enough space to write on. Labeling is important. As days pass by, it's easy enough to tell a tomato plant from a broccoli plant, but what if you planted more than one variety of tomato? One year I confused hot peppers with sweet bell peppers. The cutworm could tell the difference. He leveled all the sweet ones and left all the hot peppers alone! Obviously this was no Tex-Mex cutworm.

IN THE BEGINNING THERE WAS A GARDEN

The first little garden I ever planted many years ago was a total disaster. We were newlyweds then and I was out to prove to my beloved that I knew how to grow things. I was, after all, a farmer's daughter! So I searched through the garage for my hoe and spent the next hour chipping away at the soil next to the foundation by the back of the house. The hot sun was beating down and I was quickly getting warm and tired, so I figured enough was enough. It was time to plant. Out of the house I came, proudly showing off my flowering geraniums and petunias. With a flick of my trowel they went into the ground. All summer long I waited for them to bloom and flourish. Flourish they did not! It wasn't until I had read up on gardening and soils some time later that I realized where I had gone wrong. Plants need more than our will and good intentions to thrive. They need nutrients from good soil along with adequate moisture and sun or shade.

Mistakes can lead us down the path of learning although it's often painful and time-consuming. If you're ready to start a new garden plot this spring, keep these suggestions in mind so you don't make the same mistakes that I made when I was starting out. We can start a garden bed any season of the year but in our part of the country, we know that winter is ruled out. Many of us wait for spring, the time for fresh beginnings. If we have lots of decomposed organic material around to add to our soil, we can have a garden ready for spring planting IF our energy level holds up.

Let's start with the site. Where do you want to put your garden? Is your yard open with lots of sunshine or is it mostly shaded by groves of trees? Most vegetables need a full day of sunshine to flourish but flowers give us more options. Shaded flower gardens can be lovely and there are many species of flowers that we can choose that need only a few hours of sun, or even no direct sunshine at all. Will you be able to see your garden from inside your house or as you cruise up your driveway? Gardens are for viewing. Let's put them where we can keep an eye on them and not hide them out in the far-off edge of the yard. The small flower garden behind our house has given me lots of pleasure these past years. As I'm up to my elbows in suds from the kitchen sink, I can glance out the window and see birds flapping in the birdbath, and watch the colors of the irises and poppies unfold. It always gives me a lift.

Does the site drain well, or does water collect there after a rain? Few plants can exist for long if their roots are soaking in puddles of water. Take a soil test so you know the pH of the soil. Is it in the neutral zone (6 1/2 to 7) where most plants thrive or is it really acidic or alkaline?

Draw up a plan that includes the size and shape of the plot and a few of the plants you want to include. Hostas, ferns and bleeding hearts do well in the shade but peonies, irises and poppies need lots of sunshine. Know the requirements of the plants you choose or you'll be disappointed when they don't grow. Start small. Creating a new garden takes lots of patience and back-breaking work. What looks like a piece of cake on paper suddenly becomes a huge project once you start outside, so don't bite off more than you can chew.

Once the plan is on paper, it's time to go outdoors and start putting these ideas to work. Take a supple garden hose and snake it around until it assumes the shape of the plot you have in mind. Curved lines and round shapes are the most pleasing to the eye. The old rectangular flower bed pressed up against the yard fence is old hat. Once the shape is decided, it's time to cut all around the edge and remove the sod. This is a good job for husbands! Unfortunately, about this time, they're off running errands or fishing. All of the bending, pushing, pulling and hauling that goes with this job requires lots of coffee breaks. Take it easy and don't plan to get it all done in one day.

Put a heavy-duty tarp next to the plot for collection of sod. After a few hours of drying under the warm sun, it will be easier to shake off the extra soil from the sod and include this with the top soil later on. What's left after shaking dirt from the sod goes in my compost pile.

The next step is almost as much work as lifting sod, and I know we all would like to skip it. But we can't! This step will determine the fate of the plants that will be growing in this garden. Remove the next 6 to 8 inches of topsoil and set it alongside the bed. We'll get back to it later. Then add compost and other organic material such as decayed leaves, aged manure, old grass clippings, or seaweed. Mix this in about 8 to10 inches using a spading fork or a garden tiller. This organic matter will help hold moisture and make food available to the plants for several years to come. Rake the plot level once you've worked this organic matter in well.

Now is the time to return the top soil and any dirt shaken from the sod to the plot. Add peat moss if the soil is sandy to improve its water-holding capacity. Peat added to heavy clay soil will loosen it and improve drainage. Add any edging you want while the soil is still soft. There are lots of possibilities here: old bricks, railroad ties, stones, or conventional garden edging. All of these will help hold back the invading grass/weeds Also add any walkways or stepping stones. We certainly don't want to pack it down by stepping all around in it after we've worked so hard to loosen it up! Planting time is finally here. If you follow these steps, I guarantee you'll have a much better garden than the first one I attempted twenty years ago.

For those early bird gardeners who can't resist the temptation to garden before Memorial Day, black plastic laid over freshly tilled soil will warm the soil and give plants a better start.

If your compost pile has thawed out and is only partially rotted, sprinkle it generously with nitrogen and turn it over with a shovel. This dose of nitrogen plus the ventilation from turning it will encourage decomposition. It may even be ready for some late planting in June.